The Poetry of James Thomson

Volume II (of III) – The Castle of Indolence & Liberty

James Thomson was born in Ednam in Roxburghshire around 11th September 1700 and baptised on 15th September. He was the fourth of nine children to father Thomas, the Presbyterian minister of Ednam and mother Beatrix.

Apart from the exact date of his birth several other facts of his life cannot be verified.

It is thought Thomson may have attended the parish school of Southdean, his father having been appointed minster there a few months after the birth of his son, before attending the grammar school in Jedburgh in 1712. Accounts of his early abilities are almost always negative. Poetry however was his great love. In this he was encouraged by Robert Riccaltoun, a farmer, poet and Presbyterian minister; and Sir William Bennet, a whig laird who was also the patron of Allan Ramsay. Very few early poems by Thomson survive. It seems that on each New Year's Day he burned almost all of his year's output.

In the autumn of 1715 he entered the College of Edinburgh on a career path that would take him to the Presbyterian ministry. In college he studied metaphysics, Logic, Ethics, Greek, Latin and Natural Philosophy. He also became a member of the Grotesque Club, a literary group. Here he met his lifelong friend to be; David Mallet.

In 1716 his father, Thomas, died. Again, facts are hard to come by but there is a colourful local legend that he died whilst performing an exorcism.

In 1719 Thomson completed his arts course but rather than graduate he instead entered Divinity Hall to become a minister.

However Thomson was also keen on literary pursuits. He managed to obtain publication of several of his poems in the 'Edinburgh Miscellany'. With this as his calling card he followed Mallet to London in February 1725 in an attempt at further publishing success. For Thomson a career as a minister was now behind him.

In London, Thomson became a tutor to the son of Charles Hamilton, Lord Binning, via connections on his mother's side of the family. Through David Mallet, who by 1724 was now also a published poet, Thomson met the great English poets of the day including Richard Savage, Aaron Hill and Alexander Pope.

Beatrix, Thomson's mother died on 12th May 1725, around the time of his writing 'Winter', the first poem of 'The Seasons'. 'Winter' was first published by John Millian in 1726 with a second edition incorporating revisions, additions and a preface later that same year.

By 1727, Thomson was working on 'Summer', which he published in February, whilst working at Watt's Academy, a school for young gentlemen and a centre of Newtonian science.

That same year Millian published Thomson's 'A Poem to the Memory of Sir Isaac Newton' in memory of the great scientist who had passed in March.

Thomson now left Watt's academy hoping to further pursue his career. This was greatly helped by finding several patrons including Thomas Rundle, the countess of Hertford and Charles Talbot, 1st Baron Talbot.

Thomson worked hard to complete 'The Seasons' during the late 1720's. 'Spring' was completed in 1728 and finally Autumn in 1730. Now the complete set of four could be published together as 'The Seasons'.

During this period he also wrote other poems, as well as a play, his first, 'The Tragedy of Sophonisba' in 1729. The latter is best known today for its mention in Samuel Johnson's Lives of the English Poets, where Johnson records that one 'feeble' line of the poem – "O, Sophonisba, Sophonisba, O!" was parodied by the wags of the theatre as, "O, Jemmy Thomson, Jemmy Thomson, O!"

In 1730, he was appointed tutor to the son of Sir Charles Talbot, his patron and also Solicitor-General. Thomson would spend nearly two years with the young man on 'the grand tour' of Europe. On his return Talbot graciously arranged for Thomson to become a secretary in chancery, which gave him financial security during until Talbot's death in 1737. Meanwhile, in 1734 Thomson's major work 'Liberty' was published.

In 1740, he collaborated with Mallet on the masque 'Alfred' which was first performed at Cliveden, the country home of Frederick, Prince of Wales. Thomson's words for 'Rule Britannia', from that masque, and set to music by Thomas Arne, became one of the best-known British patriotic songs. The Prince settled on him a pension of £100 per annum. He also introduced him to George Lyttelton, who became his friend and patron.

In later years, Thomson lived in Richmond upon Thames, and it was there that he wrote his final work 'The Castle of Indolence', which was published just before his untimely death on 27th August 1748. Johnson writes on Thomson's death that "by taking cold on the water between London and Kew, he caught a disorder, which, with some careless exasperation, ended in a fever that put end to his life".

He was buried in St. Mary Magdalene church in Richmond.

Index of Poems

THE CASTLE OF INDOLENCE: AN ALLEGORICAL POEM

First published in 1748; first ed. in 4to, and second in 8vo, both in the same year. Thomson died in the following August, about four months after the appearance of this exquisite poem. The text of the second edition, as being the last to receive the author's revision, is given here.

ADVERTISEMENT

This Poem being writ in the manner of Spenser, the obsolete words, and a simplicity of diction in some of the lines which borders on the ludicrous, were necessary to make the imitation more perfect, And the style of that admirable poet, as well as the measure in which he wrote, are as it were appropriated by custom to all allegorical poems writ in our language—just as in French the style of Marot, who lived under Francis I, has been used in tales and familiar epistles by the politest writers of the age of Louis XIV.

THE CASTLE OF INDOLENCE

CANTO I

The Castle hight at Indolence,
And its false luxury;
Where for a little time, alas!
We lived right jollily.

I

O mortal man, who livest here by toil,
Do not complain of this thy hard estate;
That like an emmet thou must ever moil
Is a sad sentence of an ancient date:
And, certes, there is for it reason great;
For, though sometimes it makes thee weep and wail,
And curse thy stars, and early drudge and late,
Withouten that would come an heavier bale,
Loose life, unruly passions, and diseases pale.

II

In lowly dale, fast by a river's side,
With woody hill o'er hill encompassed round,
A most enchanting wizard did abide,
Than whom a fiend more fell is nowhere found.
It was, I ween, a lovely spot of ground;
And there a season atween June and May,
Half prankt with spring, with summer half imbrowned,
A listless climate made, where, sooth to say,
No living wight could work, ne cared even for play.

III

Was nought around but images of rest:
Sleep-soothing groves, and quiet lawns between;
And flowery beds that slumbrous influence kest,
From poppies breathed; and beds of pleasant green,
Where never yet was creeping creature seen.
Meantime unnumbered glittering streamlets played,
And hurled everywhere their waters sheen;
That, as they bickered through the sunny glade,
Though restless still themselves, a lulling murmur made.

IV

Joined to the prattle of the purling rills,
Were heard the lowing herds along the vale,
And flocks loud-bleating from the distant hills,
And vacant shepherds piping in the dale:
And now and then sweet Philomel would wail,
Or stock-doves plain amid the forest deep,
That drowsy rustled to the sighing gale;
And still a coil the grasshopper did keep:
Yet all these sounds yblent inclined all to sleep.

V

Full in the passage of the vale, above,
A sable, silent, solemn forest stood;
Where nought but shadowy forms were seen to move,
As Idless fancied in her dreaming mood.
And up the hills, on either side, a wood
Of blackening pines, ay waving to and fro,

Sent forth a sleepy horror through the blood;
And where this valley winded out, below,
The murmuring main was heard, and scarcely heard, to flow.

VI

A pleasing land of drowsyhed it was:
Of dreams that wave before the half-shut eye;
And of gay castles in the clouds that pass,
For ever flushing round a summer sky:
There eke the soft delights, that witchingly
Instil a wanton sweetness through the breast,
And the calm pleasures always hovered nigh;
But whate'er smacked of noyance, or unrest,
Was far far off expelled from this delicious nest.

VII

The landskip such, inspiring perfect ease;
Where INDOLENCE(for so the wizard hight)
Close-hid his castle mid embowering trees,
That half shut out the beams of Phoebus bright,
And made a kind of checkered day and night.
Meanwhile, unceasing at the massy gate,
Beneath a spacious palm, the wicked wight
Was placed; and, to his lute, of cruel fate
And labour harsh complained, lamenting man's estate.

VIII

Thither continual pilgrims crowded still
From all the roads of earth that pass there by:
For, as they chaunced to breathe on neighbouring hill,
The freshness of this valley smote their eye,
And drew them ever and anon more nigh,
Till clustering round the enchanter false they hung,
Ymolten with his syren melody;
While o'er th' enfeebling lute his hand he flung,
And to the trembling chord these tempting verses sung:

IX

'Behold! ye pilgrims of this earth, behold!
See all but man with unearned pleasure gay.

See her bright robes the butterfly unfold,
Broke from her wintry tomb in prime of May.
What youthful bride can equal her array?
Who can with her for easy pleasure vie?
From mead to mead with gentle wing to stray,
From flower to flower on balmy gales to fly,
Is all she has to do beneath the radiant sky.

X

'Behold the merry minstrels of the morn,
The swarming songsters of the careless grove,
Ten thousand throats that, from the flowering thorn,
Hymn their good God, and carol sweet of love,
Such grateful kindly raptures them emove!
They neither plough nor sow; ne, fit for flail,
E'er to the barn the nodding sheaves they drove
Yet theirs each harvest dancing in the gale,
Whatever crowns the hill, or smiles along the vale.

XI

'Outcast of Nature, man! the wretched thrall
Of bitter-dropping sweat, of sweltry pain,
Of cares that eat away thy heart with gall,
And of the vices, an inhuman train,
That all proceed from savage thirst of gain:
For when hard-hearted Interest first began
To poison earth, Astraea left the plain;
Guile, Violence, and Murder seized on man,
And, for soft milky streams, with blood the rivers ran.

XII

'Come, ye, who still the cumbrous load of life
Push hard up hill; but, as the farthest steep
You trust to gain, and put an end to strife,
Down thunders back the stone with mighty sweep,
And hurls your labours to the valley deep,
Forever vain: come, and withouten fee
I in oblivion will your sorrows steep,
Your cares, your toils; will steep you in a sea
Of full delight: O come, ye weary wights, to me!

XIII

'With me, you need not rise at early dawn,
To pass the joyless day in various stounds;
Or, louting low, on upstart fortune fawn,
And sell fair honour for some paltry pounds;
Or through the city take your dirty rounds
To cheat, and dun, and lie, and visit pay,
Now flattering base, now giving secret wounds;
Or prowl in courts of law for human prey,
In venal senate thieve, or rob on broad highway.

XIV

'No cocks, with me, to rustic labour call,
From village on to village sounding clear;
To tardy swain no shrill-voiced matrons squall;
No dogs, no babes, no wives to stun your ear;
No hammers thump; no horrid blacksmith sear,
Ne noisy tradesman your sweet slumbers start
With sounds that are a misery to hear:
But all is calm as would delight the heart
Of Sybarite of old, all nature, and all art.

XV

'Here nought but candour reigns, indulgent ease,
Good-natured lounging, sauntering up and down:
They who are pleased themselves must always please;
On others' ways they never squint a frown,
Nor heed what haps in hamlet or in town.
Thus, from the source of tender Indolence,
With milky blood the heart is overflown,
Is soothed and sweetened by the social sense;
For interest, envy, pride, and strife are banished hence.

XVI

'What, what is virtue but repose of mind?
A pure ethereal, calm that knows no storm,
Above the reach of wild ambition's wind,
Above those passions that this world deform,
And torture man, a proud malignant worm!
But here, instead, soft gales of passion play,
And gently stir the heart, thereby to form

A quicker sense of joy; as breezes stray
Across the enlivened skies, and make them still more gay.

XVII

'The best of men have ever loved repose:
They hate to mingle in the filthy fray;
Where the soul sours, and gradual rancour grows,
Imbittered more from peevish day to day.
Even those whom fame has lent her fairest ray,
The most renowned of worthy wights of yore,
From a base world at last have stolen away:
So Scipio, to the soft Cumaean shore
Retiring, tasted joy he never knew before.

XVIII

'But if a little exercise you chuse,
Some zest for ease, 'tis not forbidden here.
Amid the groves you may indulge the muse,
Or tend the blooms, and deck the vernal year;
Or softly stealing, with your watery gear,
Along the brooks, the crimson-spotted fry
You may delude: the whilst, amused, you hear
Now the hoarse stream, and now the zephyr's sigh,
Attuned to the birds, and woodland melody.

XIX

'O grievous folly! to heap up estate,
Losing the days you see beneath the sun;
When, sudden, comes blind unrelenting fate,
And gives the untasted portion you have won
With ruthless toil, and many a wretch undone,
To those who mock you gone to Pluto's reign,
There with sad ghosts to pine, and shadows dun:
But sure it is of vanities most vain,
To toil for what you here untoiling may obtain.'

XX

He ceased. But still their trembling ears retained
The deep vibrations of his witching song;
That, by a kind of magic power, constrained

To enter in, pell-mell, the listening throng.
Heaps poured on heaps, and yet they slipt along
In silent ease: as when, beneath the beam
Of summer moons, the distant woods among,
Or by some flood all silvered with the gleam,
The soft-embodied fays through airy portal stream.

XXI

By the smooth demon so it ordered was,
And here his baneful bounty first began:
Though some there were who would not further pass,
And his alluring baits suspected han.
The wise distrust the too fair-spoken man.
Yet through the gate they cast a wishful eye:
Not to move on, perdie, is all they can;
For, do their very best, they cannot fly,
But often each way look, and often sorely sigh.

XXII

When this the watchful wicked wizard saw,
With sudden spring he leaped upon them strait;
And, soon as touched by his unhallowed paw,
They found themselves within the cursed gate,
Full hard to be repassed, like that of Fate.
Not stronger were of old the giant-crew,
Who sought to pull high Jove from regal state,
Though feeble wretch he seemed, of sallow hue:
Certes, who bides his grasp, will that encounter rue.

XXIII

For whomsoe'er the villain takes in hand,
Their joints unknit, their sinews melt apace;
As lithe they grow as any willow-wand,
And of their vanished force remains no trace:
So when a maiden fair, of modest grace,
In all her buxom blooming May of charms,
Is seized in some losers hot embrace,
She waxeth very weakly as she warms,
Then sighing yields her up to love's delicious harms.

XXIV

Waked by the crowd, slow from his bench arose
A comely full-spread porter, swoln with sleep:
His calm broad, thoughtless aspect breathed repose;
And in sweet torpor he was plunged deep,
Ne could himself from ceaseless yawning keep;
While o'er his eyes the drowsy liquor ran,
Through which his half-waked soul would faintly peep.
Then, taking his black staff, he called his man,
And roused himself as much as rouse himself he can.

XXV

The lad leaped lightly at his master's call.
He was, to weet, a little roguish page,
Save sleep and play who minded nought at all,
Like most the untaught striplings of his age.
This boy he kept each band to disengage,
Garters and buckles, task for him unfit,
But ill-becoming his grave personage,
And which his portly paunch would not permit.
So this same limber page to all performed it.

XXVI

Meantime the master-porter wide displayed
Great store of caps, of slippers, and of gowns,
Wherewith he those who entered in arrayed,
Loose as the breeze that plays along the downs,
And waves the summer woods when evening frowns.
O fair undress, best dress! it checks no vein,
But every flowing limb in pleasure drowns,
And heightens ease with grace. This done, right fain
Sir Porter sat him down, and turned to sleep again.

XXVII

Thus easy robed, they to the fountain sped,
That in the middle of the court up-threw
A stream, high-spouting from its liquid bed,
And falling back again in drizzly dew:
There each deep draughts, as deep he thirsted, drew;
It was a fountain of Nepenthe rare:
Whence, as Dan Homer sings, huge pleasaunce grew,
And sweet oblivion of vile earthly care,

Fair gladsome waking thoughts, and joyous dreams more fair.

XXVIII

This rite performed, all inly pleased and still,
Withouten trump was proclamation made:
'Ye sons of Indolence, do what you will;
And wander where you list, through hall or glade:
Be no man's pleasure for another's staid:
Let each as likes him best his hours employ,
And curst be he who minds his neighbour's trade!
Here dwells kind ease, and unreproving joy:
He little merits bliss who others can annoy.'

XXIX

Strait of these endless numbers, swarming round
As thick as idle motes in sunny ray,
Not one eftsoons in view was to be found,
But every man strolled off his own glad way.
Wide o'er this ample-court's blank area,
With all the lodges that thereto pertained,
No living creature could be seen to stray;
While solitude and perfect silence reigned:
So that to think you dreamt you almost was constrained.

XXX

As when a shepherd of the Hebrid Isles,
Placed far amid the melancholy main,
(Whether it be lone fancy him beguiles,
Or that aerial beings sometimes deign
To stand embodied to our senses plain)
Sees on the naked hill, or valley low,
The whilst in ocean Phoebus dips his wain,
A vast assembly moving to and fro;
Then all at once in air dissolves the wondrous show.

XXXI

Ye gods of quiet, and of sleep profound,
Whose soft dominion o'er this castle sways,
And all the widely-silent places round,
Forgive me, if my trembling pen displays

What never yet was sung in mortal lays.
But how shall I attempt such arduous string?
I who have spent my nights and nightly days
In this soul-deadening place, loose-loitering—
Ah! how shall I for this uprear my moulted wing?

XXXII

Come on, my muse, nor stoop to low despair,
Thou imp of Jove, touched by celestial fire!
Thou yet shalt sing of war, and actions fair,
Which the bold sons of Britain will inspire;
Of ancient bards thou yet shalt sweep the lyre;
Thou yet shalt tread in tragic pall the stage,
Paint love's enchanting woes, the hero's ire,
The sage's calm, the patriot's noble rage,
Dashing corruption down through every worthless age.

XXXIII

The doors, that knew no shrill alarming bell,
Ne cursed knocker plied by villain's hand,
Self-opened into halls, where, who can tell
What elegance and grandeur wide expand
The pride of Turkey and of Persia land?
Soft quilts on quilts, on carpets carpets spread,
And couches stretched around in seemly band;
And endless pillows rise to prop the head;
So that each spacious room was one full-swelling bed.

XXXIV

And everywhere huge covered tables stood,
With wines high-flavoured and rich viands crowned
Whatever sprightly juice or tasteful food
On the green bosom of this Earth are found,
And all old Ocean genders in his round—
Some hand unseen these silently displayed,
Even undemanded by a sign or sound;
You need but wish, and, instantly obeyed,
Fair-ranged the dishes rose, and thick the glasses played.

XXXV

Here freedom reigned without the least alloy;
Nor gossip's tale, nor ancient maiden's gall,
Nor saintly spleen durst murmur at our joy,
And with envenomed tongue our pleasures pall.
For why? there was but one great rule for all;
To wit, that each should work his own desire,
And eat, drink, study, sleep, as it may fall,
Or melt the time in love, or wake the lyre,
And carol what, unbid, the Muses might inspire.

XXXVI

The rooms with costly tapestry were hung,
Where was inwoven many a gentle tale,
Such as of old the rural poets sung
Or of Arcadian or Sicilian vale:
Reclining lovers, in the lonely dale,
Poured forth at large the sweetly tortured heart;
Or, looking tender passion, swelled the gale,
And taught charmed echo to resound their smart;
While flocks, woods, streams around, repose and peace impart.

XXXVII

Those pleased the most, where, by a cunning hand,
Depeinten was the patriarchal age;
What time Dan Abraham left the Chaldee land,
And pastured on from verdant stage to stage,
Where fields and fountains fresh could best engage.
Toil was not then. Of nothing took they heed,
But with wild beasts the silvan war to wage,
And o'er vast plains their herds and flocks to feed:
Blest sons of nature they! true golden age indeed!

XXXVIII

Sometimes the pencil, in cool airy halls,
Bade the gay bloom of vernal landskips rise,
Or Autumn's varied shades imbrown the walls:
Now the black tempest strikes the astonished eyes;
Now down the steep the flashing torrent flies;
The trembling sun now plays o'er ocean blue,
And now rude mountains frown amid the skies;
Whate'er Lorrain light-touched with softening hue,
Or savage Rosa dashed, or learned Poussin drew.

XXXIX

Each sound too here to languishment inclined,
Lulled the weak bosom, and induced ease.
Aerial music in the warbling wind,
At distance rising oft, by small degrees,
Nearer and nearer came, till o'er the trees
It hung, and breathed such soul-dissolving airs
As did, alas! with soft perdition please:
Entangled deep in its enchanting snares,
The listening heart forgot all duties and all cares.

XL

A certain music, never known before,
Here soothed the pensive melancholy mind;
Full easily obtained. Behoves no more,
But sidelong to the gently-waving wind
To lay the well-tuned instrument reclined;
From which, with airy flying fingers light,
Beyond each mortal touch the most refined,
The god of winds drew sounds of deep delight:
Whence, with just cause, The Harp of Aeolus it hight.

XLI

Ah me! what hand can touch the strings so fine?
Who up the lofty diapasan roll
Such sweet, such sad, such solemn airs divine,
Then let them down again into the soul?
Now rising love they fanned; now pleasing dole
They breathed, in tender musings, through the heart;
And now a graver sacred strain they stole,
As when seraphic hands an hymn impart:
Wild warbling Nature all, above the reach of Art!

XLII

Such the gay splendour, the luxurious state,
Of Caliphs old, who on the Tygris' shore,
In mighty Bagdat, populous and great,
Held their bright court, where was of ladies store;
And verse, love, music still the garland wore:

When sleep was coy, the bard in waiting there
Cheered the lone midnight with the muse's lore;
Composing music bade his dreams be fair,
And music lent new gladness to the morning air.

XLIII

Near the pavilions where we slept, still ran
Soft-tinkling streams, and dashing waters fell,
And sobbing breezes sighed, and oft began
(So worked the wizard) wintry storms to swell,
As heaven and earth they would together mell:
At doors and windows, threatening, seemed to call
The demons of the tempest, growling fell;
Yet the least entrance found they none at all;
Whence sweeter grew our sleep, secure in massy hall.

XLIV

And hither Morpheus sent his kindest dreams,
Raising a world of gayer tinct and grace;
O'er which were shadowy cast Elysian gleams,
That played in waving lights from place to place,
And shed a roseate smile on nature's face.
Not Titian's pencil e'er could so array,
So fleece with clouds the pure ethereal space;
Ne could it e'er such melting forms display,
As loose on flowery beds all languishingly lay.

XLV

No, fair illusions! artful phantoms, no!
My muse will not attempt your fairy-land:
She has no colours that like you can glow;
To catch your vivid scenes too gross her hand.
But sure it is, was ne'er a subtler band
Than these same guileful angel-seeming sprights,
Who thus in dreams voluptuous, soft, and bland,
Poured all the Arabian heaven upon our nights,
And blessed them oft besides with more refined delights.

XLVI

They were in sooth a most enchanting train,

Even feigning virtue; skilful to unite
With evil good, and strew with pleasure pain.
But, for those fiends whom blood and broils delight,
Who hurl the wretch as if to hell outright
Down, down black gulfs where sullen waters sleep,
Or hold him clambering all the fearful night
On beetling cliffs, or pent in ruins deep—
They, till due time should serve, were bid far hence to keep.

XLVII

Ye guardian spirits, to whom man is dear,
From these foul demons shield the midnight gloom!
Angels of fancy and of love, be near,
And o'er the wilds of sleep diffuse a bloom;
Evoke the sacred shades of Greece and Rome,
And let them virtue with a look impart!
But chief, a while O! lend us from the tomb
Those long-lost friends for whom in love we smart,
And fill with pious awe and joy-mixt woe the heart!

XLVIII

Or are you sportive?—bid the morn of youth
Rise to new light, and beam afresh the days
Of innocence, simplicity, and truth,
To cares estranged, and manhood's thorny ways
What transport to retrace our boyish plays,
Our easy bliss, when each thing joy supplied—
The woods, the mountains, and the warbling maze
Of the wild brooks! But, fondly wandering wide,
My muse, resume the task that yet doth thee abide.

XLIX

One great amusement of our household was—
In a huge crystal magic globe to spy,
Still as you turned it, all things that do pass
Upon this ant-hill earth; where constantly
Of idly-busy men the restless fry
Run bustling to and fro with foolish haste
In search of pleasures vain, that from them fly,
Or which, obtained, the caitiffs dare not taste:
When nothing is enjoyed, can there be greater waste?

L

Of Vanity the Mirror this was called.
Here you a muckworm of the town might see
At his dull desk, amid his legers stalled,
Eat up with carking care and penurie,
Most like to carcase parched on gallow-tree.
'A penny saved is a penny got'—
Firm to this scoundrel maxim keepeth he,
Ne of its rigour will he bate a jot,
Till it has quenched his fire, and banished his pot.

LI

Strait from the filth of this low grub, behold!
Comes fluttering forth a gaudy spendthrift heir,
All glossy gay, enamelled all with gold,
The silly tenant of the summer-air.
In folly lost, of nothing takes he care;
Pimps, lawyers, stewards, harlots, flatterers vile,
And thieving tradesmen him among them share:
His father's ghost from Limbo-lake the while
Sees this, which more damnation doth upon him pile.

LII

This globe pourtrayed the race of learned men,
Still at their books, and turning o'er the page,
Backwards and forwards: oft they snatch the pen
As if inspired, and in a Thespian rage;
Then write, and blot, as would your ruth engage.
Why, authors, all this scrawl and scribbling sore?
To lose the present, gain the future age,
Praised to be when you can hear no more,
And much enriched with fame when useless worldly store!

LIII

Then would a splendid city rise to view,
With carts, and cars, and coaches roaring all:
Wide-poured abroad, behold the prowling crew;
See how they dash along from wall to wall!
At every door, hark how they thundering call!
Good Lord! what can this giddy rout excite?

Why? each on each to prey, by guile or gall;
With flattery these, with slander those to blight,
And make new tiresome parties for the coming night.

LIV

The puzzling sons of party next appeared,
In dark cabals and nightly juntos met;
And now they whispered close, now shrugging reared
The important shoulder; then, as if to get
New light, their twinkling eyes were inward set.
No sooner Lucifer recalls affairs,
Than forth they various rush in mighty fret;
When lo! pushed up to power, and crowned their cares,
In comes another set, and kicketh them down stairs.

LV

But what most showed the vanity of life
Was to behold the nations all on fire,
In cruel broils engaged, and deadly strife:
Most Christian kings, inflamed by black desire,
With honourable ruffians in their hire,
Cause war to rage, and blood around to pour.
Of this sad work when each begins to tire,
They sit them down just where they were before,
Till for new scenes of woe peace shall their force restore.

LVI

To number up the thousands dwelling here,
An useless were, and eke an endless task—
From kings, and those who at the helm appear,
To gipsies brown in summer-glades who bask.
Yea, many a man, perdie, I could unmask,
Whose desk and table make a solemn show
With tape-tied trash, and suits of fools, that ask
For place or pension, laid in decent row;
But these I passen by, with nameless numbers moe.

LVII

Of all the gentle tenants of the place,
There was a man of special grave remark:

A certain tender gloom o'erspread his face,
Pensive, not sad; in thought involved, not dark:
As soote this man could sing as morning-lark,
And teach the noblest morals of the heart;
But these his talents were yburied stark;
Of the fine stores he nothing would impart,
Which or boon nature gave or nature-painting art.

LVIII

To noontide shades incontinent he ran
Where purls the brook with sleep-inviting sound;
Or, when Dan Sol to slope his wheels began,
Amid the broom he basked him on the ground,
Where the wild thyme and camomil are found:
There would he linger till the latest ray
Of light sat quivering on the welkin's bound;
Then homeward through the twilight shadows stray,
Sauntering and slow. So had he passed many a day.

LIX

Yet not in thoughtless slumber were they past:
For oft the heavenly fire, that lay concealed
Emongst the sleeping embers, mounted fast,
And all its native light anew revealed.
Oft as he traversed the cerulean field,
And marked the clouds that drove before the wind,
Ten thousand glorious systems would he build,
Ten thousand great ideas filled his mind;
But with the clouds they fled, and left no trace behind.

LX

With him was sometimes joined in silent walk
(Profoundly silent, for they never spoke)
One shyer still, who quite detested talk:
Oft, stung by spleen, at once away he broke
To groves of pine and broad o'ershadowing oak;
There, inly thrilled, he wandered all alone,
And on himself his pensive fury wroke,
Ne ever uttered word, save when first shone
The glittering star of eve—'Thank heaven! the day is done,'

LXI

Here lurked a wretch who had not crept abroad
For forty years, ne face of mortal seen—
In chamber brooding like a loathly toad;
And sure his linen was not very clean.
Through secret loophole, that had practised been
Near to his bed, his dinner vile he took;
Unkempt, and rough, of squalid face and mien,
Our castle's shame! whence, from his filthy nook,
We drove the villain out for fitter lair to look.

LXII

One day there chanced into these halls to rove
A joyous youth, who took you at first sight;
Him the wild wave of pleasure hither drove,
Before the sprightly tempest tossing light:
Certes, he was a most engaging wight,
Of social glee, and wit humane though keen,
Turning the night to day and day to night:
For him the merry bells had rung, I ween,
If, in this nook of quiet, bells had ever been.

LXIII

But not even pleasure to excess is good:
What most elates then sinks the soul as low:
When spring-tide joy pours in with copious flood,
The higher still the exulting billows flow,
The farther back again they flagging go
And leave us grovelling on the dreary shore.
Taught by this son of joy, we found it so;
Who, whilst he staid, kept in a gay uproar
Our maddened Castle all, the abode of sleep no more.

LXIV

As when in prime of June a burnished fly,
Sprung from the meads, o'er which he sweeps along,
Cheered by the breathing bloom and vital sky,
Tunes up amid these airy halls his song,
Soothing at first the gay reposing throng:
And oft he sips their bowl; or, nearly drowned,
He, thence recovering, drives their beds among,

And scares their tender sleep with trump profound;
Then out again he flies, to wing his mazy round.

LXV

Another guest there was, of sense refined,
Who felt each worth,—for every worth he had;
Serene yet warm, humane yet firm his mind,
As little touched as any man's with bad:
Him through their inmost walks the Muses lad,
To him the sacred love of Nature lent;
And sometimes would he make our valley glad.
Whenas we found he would not here be pent,
To him the better sort this friendly message sent:—

LXVI

'Come, dwell with us! true son of virtue, come!
But if, alas! we cannot thee persuade
To lie content beneath our peaceful dome,
Ne ever more to quit our quiet glade;
Yet, when at last thy toils, but ill apaid,
Shall dead thy fire, and damp its heavenly spark,
Thou wilt be glad to seek the rural shade,
There to indulge the muse, and nature mark:
We then a lodge for thee will rear in Hagley Park.'

LXVII

Here whilom ligged the Esopus of the age;
But, called by fame, in soul ypricked deep,
A noble pride restored him to the stage,
And roused him like a giant from his sleep.
Even from his slumbers we advantage reap:
With double force the astonished scene he wakes,
Yet quits not nature's bounds. He knows to keep
Each due decorum: now the heart he shakes,
And now with well-urged sense the enlightened judgement takes.

LXVIII

A bard here dwelt, more fat than bard beseems
Who, void of envy, guile, and lust of gain,
On virtue still, and nature's pleasing themes,

Poured forth his unpremeditated strain,
The world forsaking with a calm disdain:
Here laughed he careless in his easy seat;
Here quaffed, encircled with the joyous train;
Oft moralizing sage; his ditty sweet
He loathed much to write, ne cared to repeat.

LXIX

Full oft by holy feet our ground was trod;
Of clerks good plenty here you mote espy.
A little, round, fat, oily man of God
Was one I chiefly marked among the fry:
He had a roguish twinkle in his eye,
And shone all glittering with ungodly dew,
If a tight damsel chanced to trippen by;
Which when observed, he shrunk into his mew,
And straight would recollect his piety anew.

LXX

Nor be forgot a tribe who minded nought
(Old inmates of the place) but state affairs:
They looked, perdie, as if they deeply thought;
And on their brow sat every nation's cares.
The world by them is parcelled out in shares,
When in the Hall of Smoke they congress hold,
And the sage berry sun-burnt Mocha bears
Has cleared their inward eye: then, smoke-enrolled,
Their oracles break forth, mysterious as of old.

LXXI

Here languid Beauty kept her pale-faced court:
Bevies of dainty dames of high degree
From every quarter hither made resort;
Where, from gross mortal care and business free,
They lay poured out in ease and luxury.
Or, should they a vain show of work assume,
Alas! and well-a-day! what can it he?
To knot, to twist, to range the vernal bloom;
But far is cast the distaff, spinning-wheel, and loom.

LXXII

Their only labour was to kill the time;
And labour-dire it is, and weary woe.
They sit, they loll, turn o'er some idle rhyme;
Then, rising sudden, to the glass they go,
Or saunter forth with tottering step and slow:
This soon too rude an exercise they find;
Strait on the couch their limbs again they throw,
Where, hours on hours, they sighing lie reclined,
And court the vapoury god soft-breathing in the wind.

LXXIII

Now must I mark the villainy we found,
But ah! too late, as shall eftsoons be shown.
A place here was, deep, dreary, under ground;
Where still our inmates, when unpleasing grown,
Diseased, and loathsome, privily were thrown.
Far from the light of heaven they languished there,
Unpitied, uttering many a bitter groan;
For of these wretches taken was no care:
Fierce fiends and hags of hell their only nurses were.

LXXIV

Alas the change! from scenes of joy and rest
To this dark den, where sickness tossed alway.
Here Lethargy, with deadly sleep opprest,
Stretched on his back a mighty lubbard lay,
Heaving his sides, and snored night and day:
To stir him from his traunce it was not eath,
And his half-opened eyne he shut straitway;
He led, I wot, the softest way to death,
And taught withouten pain and strife to yield the breath.

LXXV

Of limbs enormous, but withal unsound,
Soft-swoln, and pale, here lay the Hydropsy;
Unwieldy man! with belly monstrous round,
For ever fed with watery supply;
For still he drank, and yet he still was dry.
And moping here did Hypochondria sit,
Mother of Spleen, in robes of various dye,
Who vexed was full oft with ugly fit;

And some her frantic deemed, and some her deemed a wit.

LXXVI

A lady proud she was, of ancient blood,
Yet oft her fear her pride made crouchen low:
She felt, or fancied in her fluttering mood,
All the diseases which the spittles know,
And sought all physic which the shops bestow,
And still new leaches and new drugs would try,
Her humour ever wavering to and fro;
For sometimes she would laugh, and sometimes cry,
Then sudden waxed wroth; and all she knew not why.

LXXVII

Fast by her side a listless maiden pined,
With aching head and squeamish heart-burnings;
Pale, bloated, cold, she seemed to hate mankind,
Yet loved in secret all forbidden things.
And here the Tertian shakes his chilling wings:
The sleepless Gout here counts the crowing cocks—
A wolf now gnaws him, now a serpent stings:
Whilst Apoplexy crammed Intemperance knocks
Down to the ground at once, as butcher felleth ox.

CANTO II

The Knight of Art and Industry.
And his atchievements fair;
That, by this Castle's overthrow,
Secured, and crowned were.

I

Escaped the castle of the sire of sin,
Ah! where shall I so sweet a dwelling find?
For all around without, and all within,
Nothing save what delightful was and kind,
Of goodness savouring and a tender mind,
E'er rose to view. But now another strain,
Of doleful note, alas! remains behind:
I now must sing of pleasure turned to pain,
And of the false enchanter, Indolence, complain.

II

Is there no patron to protect the Muse,
And fence for her Parnassus' barren soil?
To every labour its reward accrues,
And they are sure of bread who swink and moil;
But a fell tribe the Aonian hive despoil,
As ruthless wasps oft rob the painful bee:
Thus, while the laws not guard that noblest toil,
Ne for the Muses other meed decree,
They praised are alone, and starve right merrily.

III

I care not, fortune, what you me deny:
You cannot rob me of free nature's grace;
You cannot shut the windows of the sky,
Through which Aurora shows her brightening face:
You cannot bar my constant feet to trace
The woods and lawns by living stream at eve.
Let health my nerves and finer fibres brace,
And I their toys to the great children leave:
Of fancy, reason, virtue, nought can me bereave.

IV

Come, then, my muse, and raise a bolder song:
Come, lig no more upon the bed of sloth,
Dragging the lazy languid line along,
Fond to begin, but still to finish loth,
Thy half-writ scrolls all eaten by the moth:
Arise, and sing that generous imp of fame
Who, with the sons of softness nobly wroth,
To sweep away this human lumber came,
Or in a chosen few to rouse the slumbering flame.

V

In Fairy-land there lived a knight of old,
Of feature stern, Selvaggio well ycleped,
A rough unpolished man, robust and bold,
But wondrous poor: he neither sowed nor reaped,
Ne stores in summer for cold winter heaped;

In hunting all his days away he wore;
Now scorched by June, now in November steeped,
Now pinched by biting January sore,
He still in woods pursued the libbard and the boar;

VI

As he one morning, long before the dawn,
Pricked through the forest to dislodge his prey,
Deep in the winding bosom of a lawn,
With wood wild-fringed, he marked a taper's ray,
That from the beating rain and wintry fray
Did to a lonely cot his steps decoy:
There, up to earn the needments of the day,
He found dame Poverty, nor fair nor coy;
Her he compressed, and filled her with a lusty boy.

VII

Amid the greenwood shade this boy was bred,
And grow at last a knight of muchel fame,
Of active mind and vigorous lustyhed,
The Knight of Arts and Industry by name.
Earth was his bed, the boughs his roof did frame;
He knew no beverage but the flowing stream;
His tasteful well-earned food the silvan game,
Or the brown fruit with which the woodlands teem:
The same to him glad summer or the winter breme.

VIII

So passed his youthly morning, void of care,
Wild as the colts that through the commons run:
For him no tender parents troubled were;
He of the forest seemed to be the son,
And certes had been utterly undone
But that Minerva pity of him took,
With all the gods that love the rural wonne,
That teach to tame the soil and rule the crook;
Ne did the sacred Nine disdain a gentle look.

IX

Of fertile genius, him they nurtured well

In every science and in every art
By which mankind the thoughtless brutes excel,
That can or use, or joy, or grace impart,
Disclosing all the powers of head and heart:
Ne were the goodly exercises spared
That brace the nerves or make the limbs alert,
And mix elastic force with firmness hard:
Was never knight on ground mote be with him compared.

X

Sometimes, with early morn, he mounted gay
The hunter-steed, exulting o'er the dale,
And drew the roseate breath of orient day:
Sometimes, retiring to the secret vale,
Yclad in steel, and bright with burnished mail,
He strained the bow, or tossed the sounding spear,
Or, darting on the goal, outstript the gale,
Or wheeled the chariot in its mid career,
Or strenuous wrestled hard with many a tough compeer.

XI

At other times he pryed through Nature's store,
Whate'er she in the ethereal round contains,
Whate'er she hides beneath her verdant floor,
The vegetable and the mineral reigns;
Or else he scanned the globe, those small domains,
Where restless mortals such a turmoil keep,
Its seas, its floods, its mountains, and its plains;
But more he searched the mind, and roused from sleep
Those moral seeds whence we heroic actions reap.

XII

Nor would he scorn to stoop from high pursuits
Of heavenly Truth, and practise what she taught.
Vain is the tree of knowledge without fruits.
Sometimes in hand the spade or plough he caught,
Forth-calling all with which boon earth is fraught;
Sometimes he plied the strong mechanic tool,
Or reared the fabric from the finest draught;
And oft he put himself to Neptune's school,
Fighting with winds and waves on the vext ocean pool.

XIII

To solace then these rougher toils he tried
To touch the kindling canvas into life;
With nature his creating pencil vied,—
With nature joyous at the mimic strife:
Or to such shapes as graced Pygmalion's wife
He hewed the marble; or with varied fire
He roused the trumpet and the martial fife,
Or bade the lute sweet tenderness inspire,
Or verses framed that well might wake Apollo's lyre.

XIV

Accomplished thus he from the woods issued,
Full of great aims and bent on bold emprise;
The work which long he in his breast had brewed
Now to perform he ardent did devise,
To-wit, a barbarous world to civilize.
Earth was till then a boundless forest wild—
Nought to be seen but savage wood and skies;
No cities nourished arts, no culture smiled,
No government, no laws, no gentle manners mild.

XV

A rugged wight, the worst of brutes, was man;
On his own wretched kind he, ruthless, preyed:
The strongest still the weakest over-ran;
In every country mighty robbers swayed,
And guile and ruffian force were all their trade.
Life was not life, but rapine, want, and woe;
Which this brave knight, in noble anger, made
To swear he would the rascal rout o'erthrow,
For, by the Powers Divine, it should no more be so!

XVI

It would exceed the purport of my song
To say how this best sun, from orient climes,
Came beaming life and beauty all along,
Before him chasing indolence and crimes.
Still, as he passed, the nations he sublimes,
And calls forth arts and virtue with his ray:

Then Egypt, Greece, and Rome their golden times
Successive had; but now in ruins grey
They lie, to slavish sloth and tyranny a prey.

XVII

To crown his toils, Sir Industry then spread
The swelling sail, and made for Britain's coast.
A sylvan life till then the natives led,
In the brown shades and greenwood forest lost,
All careless rambling where it liked them most—
Their wealth the wild-deer bouncing through the glade;
They lodged at large, and lived at Nature's cost;
Save spear and bow withouten other aid;
Yet not the Roman steel their naked breast dismayed.

XVIII

He liked the soil, he liked the clement skies,
He liked the verdant hills and flowery plains:
'Be this my great, my chosen isle! (he cries)
This—whilst my labours liberty sustains—
This Queen of Ocean all assault disdains.'
Nor liked he less the genius of the land,
To freedom apt and persevering pains,
Mild to obey, and generous to command,
Tempered by forming Heaven with kindest firmest hand.

XIX

Here by degrees his master-work arose,
Whatever arts and industry can frame,
Whatever finished agriculture knows,
Fair Queen of Arts! from heaven itself who came
When Eden flourished in unspotted fame;
And still with her sweet innocence we find,
And tender peace, and joys without a name,
That, while they rapture, tranquillize the mind;
Nature and Art at once, delight and use combined.

XX

Then towns he quickened by mechanic arts,
And bade the fervent city glow with toil;

Bade social commerce raise renowned marts,
Join land to land, and marry soil to soil,
Unite the poles, and without bloody spoil
Bring home of either Ind the gorgeous stores;
Or, should despotic rage the world embroil,
Bade tyrants tremble on remotest shores,
While o'er the encircling deep Britannia's thunder roars.

XXI

The drooping Muses then he westward called,
From the famed city by Propontis Sea,
What time the Turk the enfeebled Grecian thralled;
Thence from their cloistered walks he set them free,
And brought them to another Castalie,
Where Isis many a famous noursling breeds,
Or where old Cam soft paces o'er the lea
In pensive mood, and tunes his Doric reeds,
The whilst his flocks at large the lonely shepherd feeds.

XXII

Yet the fine arts were what he finished least.
For why? They are the quintessence of all,
The growth of labouring time, and slow increast;
Unless, as seldom chances, it should fall
That mighty patrons the coy sisters call
Up to the sunshine of uncumbered ease,
Where no rude care the mounting thought may thrall,
And where they nothing have to do but please:
Ah! gracious God! thou knowst they ask no other fees.

XXIII

But now, alas! we live too late in time:
Our patrons now even grudge that little claim,
Except to such as sleek the soothing rhyme;
And yet, forsooth, they wear Maecenas' name,
Poor sons of puffed-up vanity, not fame.
Unbroken spirits, cheer! still, still remains
The eternal patron, Liberty; whose flame,
While she protects, inspires the noblest strains.
The best and sweetest far are toil-created gains.

XXIV

Whenas the knight had framed in Britain-land
A matchless form of glorious government,
In which the sovereign laws alone command,
Laws stablished by the public free consent,
Whose majesty is to the sceptre lent—
When this great plan, with each dependent art,
Was settled firm, and to his heart's content,
Then sought he from the toilsome scene to part,
And let life's vacant eve breathe quiet through the heart.

XXV

For this he chose a farm in Deva's vale,
Where his long alleys peeped upon the main.
In this calm seat he drew the healthful gale,
Commixed the chief, the patriot, and the swain,
The happy monarch of his sylvan train!
Here, sided by the guardians of the fold,
He walked his rounds, and cheered his blest domain;
His days, the days of unstained nature, rolled
Replete with peace and joy, like patriarch's of old.

XXVI

Witness, ye lowing herds, who lent him milk;
Witness, ye flocks, whose woolly vestments far
Exceed soft India's cotton, at her silk;
Witness, with Autumn charged, the nodding car
That homeward came beneath sweet evening's star,
Or of September moons the radiance mild.
O hide thy head, abominable War!
Of crimes and ruffian idleness the child!
From heaven this life ysprung, from hell thy glories vild!

XXVII

Nor from his deep retirement banished was
The amusing cares of rural industry.
Still, as with grateful change the seasons pass,
New scenes arise, new landskips strike the eye,
And all the enlivened country beautify:
Gay plains extend where marshes slept before;
O'er recent meads the exulting streamlets fly;

Dark frowning heaths grow bright with Ceres' store;
And woods imbrown the steep, or wave along the shore.

XXVIII

As nearer to his farm you made approach,
He polished nature with a finer hand:
Yet on her beauties durst not art encroach;
'Tis art's alone these beauties to expand.
In graceful dance immingled, o'er the land
Pan, Pales, Flora, and Pomona played:
Even here, sometimes, the rude wild common fand
An happy place; where, free and unafraid,
Amid the flowering brakes each coyer creature strayed.

XXIX

But in prime vigour what can last for ay?
That soul-enfeebling wizard, Indolence,
I whilom sung, wrought in his works decay:
Spread far and wide was his curst influence;
Of public virtue much he dulled the sense,
Even much of private; eat our spirit out,
And fed our rank luxurious vices: whence
The land was overlaid with many a lout;
Not, as old fame reports, wise, generous, bold, and stout.

XXX

A rage of pleasure maddened every breast;
Down to the lowest lees the ferment ran:
To his licentious wish each must be blest,
With joy be fevered,-snatch it as he can.
Thus Vice the standard reared; her arrier-ban
Corruption called, and loud she gave the word:—
'Mind, mind yourselves! why should the vulgar man,
The lacquey, be more virtuous than his lord?
Enjoy this span of life! 'tis all the gods afford.'

XXXI

The tidings reached to where in quiet hall
The good old knight enjoyed well-earned repose:
'Come, come, Sir Knight! thy children on thee call;

Come, save us yet, ere ruin round us close!
The demon Indolence thy toils o'erthrows.'
On this the noble colour stained his cheeks,
Indignant glowing through the whitening snows
Of venerable eld; his eye full-speaks
His ardent soul, and from his couch at once he breaks.

XXXII

'I will (he cried), so help me God! destroy
That villain Archimage.'—His page then strait
He to him called a fiery-footed boy
Benempt Dispatch. 'My steed be at the gate;
My bard attend; quick, bring the net of fate.'
This net was twisted by the Sisters Three;
Which, when once cast o'er hardened wretch, too late
Repentance comes: replevy cannot be
From the strong iron grasp of vengeful destiny.

XXXIII

He came, the bard, a little Druid wight,
Of withered aspect; but his eye was keen,
With sweetness mixed. In russet brown bedight,
As is his sister of the copses green,
He crept along, unpromising of mien.
Gross he who judges so. His soul was fair;
Bright as the children of yon azure sheen,
True comeliness, which nothing can impair,
Dwells in the mind: all else is vanity and glare.

XXXIV

'Come,' quoth the knight; 'a voice has reached mine ear:
The demon Indolence threats overthrow
To all that to mankind is good and dear.
Come, Philomelus, let us instant go
O'erturn his bowers and lay his castle low.
Those men, those wretched men, who will be slaves,
Must drink a bitter wrathful cup of woe:
But some there be thy song, as from their graves,
Shall raise. Thrice happy he who without rigour saves!'

XXXV

Issuing forth, the knight bestrode his steed
Of ardent bay, and on whose front a star
Shone blazing bright: sprung from the generous breed
That whirl of active Day the rapid car,
He pranced along, disdaining gate or bar,
Meantime, the bard on milk-white palfrey rode;
An honest sober beast, that did not mar
His meditations, but full softly trode:
And much they moralized as thus yfere they yode.

XXXVI

They talked of virtue, and of human bliss.
What else so fit for man to settle well?
And still their long researches met in this,
This truth of truths, which nothing can refel:—
'From virtue's fount the purest joys outwell,
Sweet rills of thought that cheer the conscious soul;
While vice pours forth the troubled streams of hell,
The which, howe'er disguised, at last with dole
Will through the tortured breast their fiery torrent roll.'

XXXVII

At length it dawned, that fatal valley gay.
O'er which high wood-crowned hills their summits rear.
On the cool height awhile our palmers stay,
And spite even of themselves their senses cheer;
Then to the wizard's wonne their steps they steer.
Like a green isle it broad beneath them spread,
With gardens round, and wandering currents clear,
And tufted groves to shade the meadow-bed,
Sweet airs and song; and without hurry all seemed glad.

XXXVIII

'As God shall judge me, Knight! we must forgive'
(The half-enraptured Philomelus cried)
'The frail good man deluded here to live,
And in these groves his musing fancy hide.
Ah, nought is pure! It cannot be denied
That virtue still some tincture has of vice,
And vice of virtue. What should then betide,
But that our charity be not too nice?

Come, let us those we can to real bliss entice.'

XXXIX

'Ay, sicker,' quoth the knight, 'all flesh is frail,
To pleasant sin and joyous dalliance bent;
But let not brutish vice of this avail,
And think to scape deserved punishment.
Justice were cruel, weakly to relent;
From Mercy's self she got her sacred glaive:
Grace be to those who can and will repent;
But penance long and dreary to the slave,
Who must in floods of fire his gross foul spirit lave.'

XL

Thus, holding high discourse, they came to where
The cursed carle was at his wonted trade;
Still tempting heedless men into his snare,
In witching wise, as I before have said.
But when he saw, in goodly gear arrayed,
The grave majestic knight approaching nigh,
And by his side the bard so sage and staid,
His countenance fell; yet oft his anxious eye
Marked them, like wily fox who roosted cock doth spy.

XLI

Nathless, with feigned respect, he bade give back
The rabble-rout, and welcomed them full kind;
Struck with the noble twain, they were not slack
His orders to obey, and fall behind.
Then he resumed his song; and unconfined
Poured all his music, ran through all his strings:
With magic dust their eyne he tries to blind,
And virtue's tender airs o'er weakness flings.
What pity, base his song who so divinely sings!

XLII

Elate in thought, he counted them his own,
They listened so intent with fixed delight:
But they instead, as if transmewed to stone,
Marvelled he could with such sweet art unite

The lights and shades of manners, wrong and right.
Meantime the silly crowd the charm devour,
Wide-pressing to the gate. Swift on the Knight
He darted fierce to drag him to his bower,
Who backening shunned his touch, for well he knew its power.

XLIII

As in thronged amphitheatre of old
The wary retiarius trapped his foe,
Even so the Knight, returning on him bold,
At once involved him in the net of woe
Whereof I mention made not long ago.
Enraged at first, he scorned so weak a jail,
And leaped, and flew, and flounced to and fro;.
But, when he found that nothing could avail,
He sat him felly down, and gnawed his bitter nail.

XLIV

Alarmed, the inferior demons of the place
Raised rueful shrieks and hideous yells around;
Black ruptured clouds deformed the welkin's face,
And from beneath was heard a wailing sound,
As of infernal sprights in cavern bound;
A solemn sadness every creature strook,
And lightnings flashed, and horror rocked the ground:
Huge crowds on crowds outpoured, with blemished look,
As if on time's last verge this frame of things had shook.

XLV

Soon as the short-lived tempest was yspent,
Steamed from the jaws of vext Avernus' hole,
And hushed the hubbub of the rabblement,
Sir Industry the first calm moment stole:
'There must,' he cried, 'amid so vast a shoal,
Be some who are not tainted at the heart,
Not poisoned quite by this same villain's bowl:
Come, then, my bard, thy heavenly fire impart;
Touch soul with soul, till forth the latent spirit start.'

XLVI

The bard obeyed; and, taking from his side,
Where it in seemly sort depending hung,
His British harp, its speaking strings he tried,
The which with skilful touch he deftly strung,
Till tinkling in clear symphony they rung.
Then, as he felt the muses come along,
Light o'er the chords his raptured hand he flung,
And played a prelude to his rising song:
The whilst, like midnight mute, ten thousands round him throng.

XLVII

Thus, ardent, burst his strain:—'Ye hapless race,
Dire-labouring here to smother reason's ray
That lights our Maker's image in our face,
And gives us wide o'er earth unquestioned sway;
What is the adored Supreme perfection? say!
What, but eternal never-resting soul,
Almighty power, and all-directing day,
By whom each atom stirs, the planets roll;
Who fills, surrounds, informs, and agitates the whole!

XLVIII

'Come, to the beaming God your hearts unfold!
Draw from its fountain life! 'Tis thence alone
We can excel. Up from unfeeling mould
To seraphs burning round the Almighty's throne,
Life rising still on life in higher tone
Perfection forms, and with perfection bliss.
In universal nature this clear shown
Not needeth proof: to prove it were, I wis,
To prove the beauteous world excels the brute abyss.

XLIX

'Is not the field, with lively culture green,
A sight more joyous than the dead morass?
Do not the skies, with active ether clean
And fanned by sprightly zephyrs, far surpass
The foul November fogs and slumbrous mass
With which sad nature veils her drooping face?
Does not the mountain stream, as clear as glass,
Gay-dancing on, the putrid pool disgrace?
The same in all holds true, but chief in human race.

L

'It was not by vile loitering in ease
That Greece obtained the brighter palm of art;
That soft yet ardent Athens learned to please,
To keen the wit, and to sublime the heart—
In all supreme! complete in every part!
It was not thence majestic Rome arose,
And o'er the nations shook her conquering dart:
For sluggard's brow the laurel never grows;
Renown is not the child of indolent repose.

LI

'Had unambitious mortals minded nought
But in loose joy their time to wear away,
Had they alone the lap of dalliance sought,
Pleased on her pillow their dull heads to lay,
Rude nature's state had been our state to-day;
No cities e'er their towery fronts had raised,
No arts had made us opulent and gay,
With brother-brutes the human race had graz'd,
None e'er had soared to fame, none honoured been, none praised.

LII

'Great Homer's song had never fired the breast
To thirst of glory and heroic deeds;
Sweet Maro's muse, sunk in inglorious rest,
Had silent slept amid the Mincian reeds:
The wits of modern time had told their beads,
And monkish legends been their only strains;
Our Milton's Eden had lain wrapt in weeds,
Our Shakespeare strolled and laughed with Warwick swains,
Ne had my master Spenser charmed his Mulla's plains.

LIII

'Dumb, too, had been the sage historic muse,
And perished all the sons of ancient fame;
Those starry lights of virtue, that diffuse
Through the dark depth of time their vivid flame,
Had all been lost with such as have no name.

Who then had scorned his ease for others' good?
Who then had toiled, rapacious men to tame?
Who in the public breach devoted stood,
And for his country's cause been prodigal of blood?

LIV

'But, should to fame your hearts impervious be,
If right I read, you pleasure all require:
Then hear how best may be obtained this fee,
How best enjoyed this nature's wide desire.
Toil, and be glad! let Industry inspire
Into your quickened limbs her buoyant breath!
Who does not act is dead; absorpt entire
In miry sloth, no pride, no joy he hath:
O leaden-hearted men, to be in love with death!

LV

'Better the toiling swain, oh happier far!
Perhaps the happiest of the sons of men!
Who vigorous plies the plough, the team, or car,
Who ploughs the field, or ditches in the glen,
Delves in his garden, or secures his pen:
The tooth of avarice poisons not his peace;
He tosses not in sloth's abhorred den;
From vanity ho has a full release;
And, rich in nature's wealth, he thinks not of increase.

LVI

'Good Lord! how keen are his sensations all!
His bread is sweeter than the glutton's cates;
The wines of France upon the palate pall
Compared with what his simple soul elates,
The native cup whose flavour thirst creates;
At one deep draught of sleep he takes the night;
And, for that heart-felt joy which nothing mates,
Of the pure nuptial bed the chaste delight,
The losel is to him a miserable wight.

LVII

'But what avail the largest gifts of Heaven,

When drooping health and spirits go amiss?
How tasteless then whatever can be given!
Health is the vital principle of bliss,
And exercise of health. In proof of this,
Behold the wretch who slugs his life away
Soon swallowed in disease's sad abyss;
While he whom toil has braced, or mauly play,
Has light as air each limb, each thought as clear as day.

LVIII

'O who can speak the vigorous joys of health?
Unclogged the body, unobscured the mind:
The morning rises gay; with pleasing stealth
The temperate evening falls serene and kind.
In health the wiser brutes true gladness find.
See how the younglings frisk along the meads
As May comes on and wakes the balmy wind!
Rampant with life, their joy all joy exceeds:
Yet what save high-strung health this dancing pleasaunce breeds?

LIX

'But here, instead, is fostered every ill
Which or distempered minds or bodies know.
Come, then, my kindred spirits! do not spill
Your talents here. This place is but a show
Whose charms delude you to the den of woe:
Come, follow me; I will direct you right,
Where pleasure's roses, void of serpents, grow,
Sincere as sweet. Come, follow this good knight;
And you will bless the day that brought him to your sight.

LX

'Some he will lead to courts, and some to camps;
To senates some, and public sage debates,
Where, by the solemn gleam of midnight lamps,
The world is poised, and managed mighty states;
To high discovery some, that new creates
The face of earth; some to the thriving mart;
Some to the rural reign, and softer fates;
To the sweet muses some, who raise the heart:
All glory shall be yours, all nature, and all art.

LXI

'There are, I see, who listen to my lay,
Who wretched sigh for virtue, but despair.
"All may be done (methinks I hear them say),
Even death despised by generous actions fair;
All: but, for those who to these bowers repair,
Their every power dissolved in luxury,
To quit of torpid sluggishness the lair
And from the powerful arms of sloth get free—
'Tis rising from the dead! Alas, it cannot be!"

LXII

'Would you then learn to dissipate the band
Of these huge threatening difficulties dire
That in the weak man's way like lions stand,
His soul appal, and damp his rising fire?
Resolve! resolve! and to be men aspire!
Exert that noblest privilege, alone
Here to mankind indulged; control desire;
Let godlike reason from her sovereign throne
Speak the commanding word "I Will!" and it is done.

LXIII

'Heavens! can you, then, thus waste in shameful wise
Your few important days of trial here?
Heirs of eternity, yborn to rise
Through endless states of being, still more near
To bliss approaching, and perfection clear—
Can you renounce a fortune so sublime,
Such glorious hopes, your backward steps to steer,
And roll, with vilest brutes, through mud and slime?
No, no!—your heaven-touched hearts disdain the sordid crime!'

LXIV

'Enough! enough!' they cried. Strait, from the crowd
The better sort on wings of transport fly—
As, when amid the lifeless summits proud
Of Alpine cliffs, where to the gelid sky
Snows piled on snows in wintry torpor lie,
The rays divine of vernal Phoebus play,

The awakened heaps, in streamlets from on high,
Roused into action, lively leap away,
Glad-warbling through the vales, in their new being gay.

LXV

Not less the life, the vivid joy serene,
That lighted up these new-created men,
Than that which wings the exulting spirit clean,
When, just delivered from this fleshly den,
It soaring seeks its native skies agen.
How light its essence! how unclogged its powers,
Beyond the blazon of my mortal pen!
Even so we glad forsook these sinful bowers;
Even such enraptured life, such energy was ours.

LXVI

But far the greater part, with rage inflamed,
Dire-muttered curses and blasphemed high Jove.
'Ye sons of hate!' (they bitterly exclaimed)
'What brought you to this seat of peace and love?
While with kind nature here amid the grove
We passed the harmless sabbath of our time,
What to disturb it could, fell men! emove
Your barbarous hearts? Is happiness a crime?
Then do the fiends of hell rule in yon Heaven sublime.'

LXVII

'Ye impious wretches,' (quoth the Knight in wrath)
'Your happiness behold!' Then strait a wand
He waved, an anti-magic power that hath
Truth from illusive falsehood to command.
Sudden the landskip sinks on every hand;
The pure quick streams are marshy puddles found;
On baleful heaths the groves all blackened stand;
And, o'er the weedy foul abhorred ground,
Snakes, adders, toads, each loathly creature crawls around.

LXVIII

And here and there, on trees by lightning scathed,
Unhappy wights who loathed life yhung;

Or in fresh gore and recent murder bathed
They weltering lay; or else, infuriate flung
Into the gloomy flood, while ravens sung
The funeral dirge, they down the torrent rolled:
These, by distempered blood to madness stung,
Had doomed themselves; whence oft, when night controlled
The world, returning hither their sad spirits howled.

LXIX

Meantime a moving scene was open laid.
That lazar-house, I whilom in my lay
Depainten have, its horrors deep-displayed,
And gave unnumbered wretches to the day,
Who tossing there in squalid misery lay.
Soon as of sacred light the unwonted smile
Poured on these living catacombs its ray,
Through the drear caverns stretching many a mile,
The sick up-raised their heads, and dropped their woes a while.

LXX

'O Heaven!' they cried, 'and do we once more see
Yon blessed sun, and this green earth so fair?
Are we from noisome damps of pest-house free?
And drink our souls the sweet ethereal air?
O thou, or knight or God, who holdest there
That fiend, oh keep him in eternal chains!
But what for us, the children of despair,
Brought to the brink of hell, what hope remains?
Repentance does itself but aggravate our pains.'

LXXI

The gentle knight, who saw their rueful case,
Let fall adown his silver beard some tears.
'Certes,' quoth he, 'it is not even in grace
To undo the past, and eke your broken years:
Nathless, to nobler worlds repentance rears
With humble hope her eye; to her is given
A power the truly contrite heart that cheers;
She quells the brand by which the rocks are riven;
She more than merely softens, she rejoices Heaven.

LXXII

'Then patient bear the sufferings you have earned,
And by these sufferings purify the mind;
Let wisdom be by past misconduct learned:
Or pious die, with penitence resigned;
And to a life more happy and refined
Doubt not you shall, new creatures, yet arise.
Till then, you may expect in me to find
One who will wipe your sorrow from your eyes,
One who will soothe your pangs, and wing you to the skies.'

LXXIII

They silent heard, and poured their thanks in tears.
'For you (resumed the Knight, with sterner tone)
Whose hard dry hearts the obdurate demon sears—
That villain's gifts will cost you many a groan;
In dolorous mansion long you must bemoan
His fatal charms, and weep your stains away;
Till, soft and pure as infant goodness grown,
You feel a perfect change: then, who can say
What grace may yet shine forth in Heaven's eternal day?'

LXXIV

This said, his powerful wand he waved anew:
Instant, a glorious angel-train descends,
The charities, to-wit, of rosy hue:
Sweet love their looks a gentle radiance lends,
And with seraphic flame compassion blends.
At once delighted to their charge they fly:
When lo! a goodly hospital ascends,
In which they bade each human aid be nigh,
That could the sick-bed smoothe of that unhappy fry.

LXXV

It was a worthy edifying sight,
And gives to human-kind peculiar grace,
To see kind hands attending day and night
With tender ministry from place to place.
Some prop the head; some from the pallid face
Wipe off the faint cold dews weak nature sheds;
Some reach the healing draught: the whilst, to chase

The fear supreme, around their softened beds,
Some holy man by prayer all opening heaven dispreads,

LXXVI

Attended by a glad acclaiming train
Of those he rescued had from gaping hell,
Then turned the knight; and, to his hall again
Soft-pacing, sought of Peace the mossy cell.
Yet down his cheeks the gems of pity fell,
To see the helpless wretches that remained,
There left through delves and deserts dire to yell:
Amazed, their looks with pale dismay were stained,
And, spreading wide their hands, they meek repentance feigned.

LXXVII

But ah! their scorned day of grace was past:
For (horrible to tell!) a desert wild
Before them stretched, bare, comfortless, and vast;
With gibbets, bones, and carcases defiled.
There nor trim field nor lively culture smiled;
Nor waving shade was seen, nor fountain fair:
But sands abrupt on sands lay loosely piled,
Through which they floundering toiled with painful care,
Whilst Phoebus smote them sore, and fired the Cloudless air.

LXXVIII

Then, varying to a joyless land of bogs,
The saddened country a gray waste appeared,
Where nought but putrid steams and noisome fogs
For ever hung on drizzly Auster's beard;
Or else the ground, by piercing Caurus seared,
Was jagged with frost or heaped with glazed snow:
Through these extremes a ceaseless round they steered,
By cruel fiends still hurried to and fro,
Gaunt Beggary, and Scorn, with many hell-hounds moe.

LXXIX

The first was with base dunghill rags yclad,
Tainting the gale in which they fluttered light;
Of morbid hue his features, sunk and sad;

His hollow eyne shook forth a sickly light;
And o'er his lank jawbone, in piteous plight,
His black rough beard was matted rank and vile;
Direful to see! a heart-appalling sight!
Meantime foul scurf and blotches him defile;
And dogs, where'er he went, still barked all the while.

LXXX

The other was a fell despightful fiend—
Hell holds none worse in baleful bower below;
By pride, and wit, and rage, and rancour keened;
Of man, alike if good or bad, the foe;
With nose upturned, he always made a show
As if he smelt some nauseous scent; his eye
Was cold and keen, like blast from boreal snow
And taunts he casten forth most bitterly.
Such were the twain that off drove this ungodly fry.

LXXXI

Even so through Brentford town, a town of mud,
An herd of bristly swine is pricked along;
The filthy beasts, that never chew the cud,
Still grunt, and squeak, and sing their troublous song,
And oft they plunge themselves the mire among;
But ay the ruthless driver goads them on,
And ay of barking dogs the bitter throng
Makes them renew their unmelodious moan;
Ne ever find they rest from their unresting fone.

LIBERTY: A POEM IN FIVE PARTS

[First published 1735 and 1736. The text here followed bears date 1738]

TO HIS ROYAL HIGHNESS FREDERICK, PRINCE OF WALES

SIR,

When I reflect upon that ready condescension, that preventing generosity, with which your Royal Highness received the following poem under your protection, I can alone ascribe it to the recommendation and influence of the subject. In you the cause and concerns of Liberty have so zealous a patron, as entitles whatever may have the least tendency to promote them to the distinction of your favour. And who can entertain this delightful reflection without feeling a pleasure far superior to that of the fondest author, and of which all true lovers of their country must participate? To behold the noblest dispositions of the prince and of the patriot united—an overflowing benevolence, generosity, and candour of heart joined to an enlightened zeal for Liberty, an intimate persuasion that on it depends the happiness and glory both of kings and people—to see these shining out in public virtues, as they have hitherto smiled in all the social lights and private accomplishments of life, is a prospect that cannot but inspire a general sentiment of satisfaction and gladness, more easy to be felt than expressed.

If the following attempt to trace Liberty from the first ages down to her excellent establishment in Great Britain can at all merit your approbation, and prove an entertainment to your Royal Highness; if it can in any degree answer the dignity of the subject, and of the name under which I presume to shelter it—I have my best reward, particularly as it affords me an opportunity of declaring that I am, with the greatest zeal and respect,

SIR,

Your Royal Highness's most obedient and most devoted servant,

JAMES THOMSON.

LIBERTY

THE CONTENTS OF PART I

The following Poem is thrown into the form of a Poetical Vision. Its scene the ruins of ancient Rome. The Goddess of Liberty, who is supposed to speak through the whole, appears, characterized as British Liberty, to verse 44. Gives a view of ancient Italy, and particularly of Republican Rome, in all her magnificence and glory, to verse 106. This contrasted by modern Italy, its valleys, mountains, culture, cities, people; the difference appearing strongest in the capital city, Rome, to verse 227. The ruins of the great works of Liberty more magnificent than the borrowed pomp of Oppression; and from them revived Sculpture, Painting, and Architecture, to verse 249. The old Romans apostrophized, with regard to the several melancholy changes in Italy: Horace, Tully, and Virgil, with regard to their Tibur, Tusculum, and Naples, to verse 285. That once finest and most ornamented part of Italy, all along the coast of Baiae, how changed, to verse 315. This desolation of Italy applied to Britain, to verse 338. Address to the Goddess of Liberty, that she would deduce from the first ages, her chief establishments, the description of which constitutes the subject of the following parts of this Poem. She assents, and commands what she says to be sung in Britain; whose happiness, arising from freedom and a limited monarchy, she marks, to verse 378. An immediate Vision attends, and paints her words. Invocation.

PART I

ANCIENT AND MODERN ITALY COMPARED

[First published early in 1735]

O my lamented Talbot! while with thee
The muse gay roved the glad Hesperian round,
And drew the inspiring breath of ancient arts;
Ah! little thought she her returning verse
Should sing our darling subject to thy shade.
And does the mystic veil, from mortal beam,
Involve those eyes where every virtue smiled,
And all thy father's candid spirit shone?
The light of reason, pure, without a cloud;
Full of the generous heart, the mild regard;
Honour disdaining blemish, cordial faith,
And limpid truth, that looks the very soul.
But to the death of mighty nations turn
My strain; be there absorbed the private tear.
Musing, I lay; warm from the sacred walks,
Where at each step imagination burns:
While scattered wide around, awful, and hoar,
Lies, a vast monument, once glorious Rome,
The tomb of empire! ruins! that efface
Whate'er, of finished, modern pomp can boast.

Snatched by these wonders to that world where thought
Unfettered ranges, fancy's magic hand
Led me anew o'er all the solemn scene,
Still in the mind's pure eye more solemn dressed:
When straight, methought, the fair majestic power
Of Liberty appeared. Not, as of old,
Extended in her hand the cap, and rod,
Whose slave-enlarging 'touch gave double life:
But her bright temples bound with British oak,
And naval honours nodded on her brow.
Sublime of port: loose o'er her shoulder flowed
Her sea-green robe, with constellations gay.
An island-goddess now; and her high care
The queen of isles, the mistress of the main.
My heart beat filial transport at the sight;
And, as she moved to speak, the awakened muse
Listened intense. Awhile she looked around,
With mournful eye the well-known ruins marked,
And then, her sighs repressing, thus began:

'Mine are these wonders, all thou seest is mine;
But ah, how changed! the falling poor remains
Of what exalted once the Ausonian shore.
Look back through time; and, rising from the gloom,
Mark the dread scene, that paints whate'er I say.

'The great republic see! that glowed, sublime,

With the mixed freedom of a thousand states;
Raised on the thrones of kings her curule chair,
And by her fasces awed the subject world.
See busy millions quickening all the land,
With cities thronged, and teeming culture high:
For nature then smiled on her free-born sons,
And poured the plenty that belongs to men.
Behold, the country cheering, villas rise
In lively prospect by the secret lapse
Of brooks now lost, and streams renowned in song;
In Umbria's closing vales, or on the brow
Of her brown hills that breathe the scented gale;
On Baia's viny coast, where peaceful seas,
Fanned by kind zephyrs, ever kiss the shore,
And suns unclouded shine, through purest air;
Or in the spacious neighbourhood of Rome,
Far shining upward to the Sabine hills,
To Anio's roar, and Tibur's olive shade,
To where Preneste lifts her airy brow,
Or downwards spreading to the sunny shore
Where Alba breathes the freshness of the main.

'See distant mountains leave their valleys dry,
And o'er the proud arcade their tribute pour,
To lave imperial Rome. For ages laid,
Deep, massy, firm, diverging every way,
With tombs of heroes sacred, see her roads—
By various nations trod and suppliant kings,
With legions flaming or with triumph gay.

'Full in the centre of these wondrous works,
The pride of earth! Rome in her glory see!
Behold her demigods, in senate met;
All head to counsel, and all heart to act:
The commonweal inspiring every tongue
With fervent eloquence, unbribed, and bold;
Ere tame corruption taught the servile herd
To rank obedient to a master's voice.

'Her forum see, warm, popular, and loud,
In trembling wonder hushed, when the two sires,
As they the private father greatly quelled,
Stood up the public fathers of the state.
See justice judging there, in human shape.
Hark! how with freedom's voice it thunders high,
Or in soft murmurs sinks to Tully's tongue.

'Her tribes, her census, see; her generous troops,

Whose pay was glory, and their best reward
Free for their country and for me to die;
Ere mercenary murder grew a trade.

'Mark, as the purple triumph waves along,
The highest pomp and lowest fall of life.

'Her festive games, the school of heroes, see;
Her circus, ardent with contending youth;
Her streets, her temples, palaces, and baths,
Full of fair forms, of beauty's eldest born,
And of a people cast in virtue's mould—
While sculpture lives around, and Asian hills
Lend their best stores to heave the pillared dome;
All that to Roman strength the softer touch
Of Grecian art can join. But language fails
To paint this sun, this centre of mankind;
Where every virtue, glory, treasure, art,
Attracted strong, in heightened lustre met.

'Need I the contrast mark? unjoyous view!
A land in all, in government and arts,
In virtue, genius, earth, and heaven, reversed.
Who but these far-famed ruins to behold, no
Proofs of a people, whose heroic aims
Soared far above the little selfish sphere
Of doubting modern life—who but inflamed
With classic zeal, these consecrated scenes
Of men and deeds to trace, unhappy land!
Would trust thy wilds and cities loose of sway?

'Are these the vales that once exulting states
In their warm bosom fed? The mountains these,
On whose high-blooming sides my sons of old
I bred to glory? These dejected towns,
Where, mean and sordid, life can scarce subsist,
The scenes of ancient opulence and pomp?

'Come! by whatever sacred name disguised,
Oppression, come! and in thy works rejoice!
See nature's richest plains to putrid fens
Turned by thy fury. From their cheerful bounds,
See razed the enlivening village, farm, and seat.
First, Rural Toil, by thy rapacious hand
Robbed of his poor reward, resigned the plough;
And now he dares not turn the noxious glebe.

'Tis thine entire. The lonely swain himself,

Who loves at large along the grassy downs
His flocks to pasture, thy drear champaign flies
Far as the sickening eye can sweep around,
'Tis all one desert, desolate, and grey,
Grazed by the sullen buffalo alone;
And, where the rank uncultivated growth
Of rotting ages taints the passing gale,
Beneath the baleful blast the city pines,
Or sinks enfeebled, or infected burns.
Beneath it mourns the solitary road,
Rolled in rude mazes o'er the abandoned waste;
While ancient ways, ingulfed, are seen no more.

'Such thy dire plains, thou self-destroyer! foe
To humankind! Thy mountains, too, profuse
Where savage nature blooms, seem their sad plaint
To raise against thy desolating rod.
There on the breezy brow, where thriving states
And famous cities once to the pleased sun
Far other scenes of rising culture spread,
Pale shine thy ragged towns. Neglected round,
Each harvest pines; the livid, lean produce
Of heartless labour: while thy hated joys,
Not proper pleasure, lift the lazy hand.
Better to sink in sloth the woes of life,
Than wake their rage with unavailing toil.
Hence drooping art almost to nature leaves
The rude unguided year. Thin wave the gifts
Of yellow Ceres, thin the radiant blush
Of orchard reddens in the warmest ray.
To weedy wildness run, no rural wealth
(Such as dictators fed) the garden pours.
Crude the wild olive flows, and foul the vine;
Nor juice Caecubian nor Falernian more
Streams life and joy, save in the muse's bowl
Unseconded by art, the spinning race
Draw the bright thread in vain, and idly toil.
In vain, forlorn in wilds, the citron blows;
And flowering plants perfume the desert gale.
Through the vile thorn the tender myrtle twines.
Inglorious droops the laurel, dead to song,
And long a stranger to the hero's brow.

'Nor half thy triumph this: cast, from brute fields,
Into the haunts of men thy ruthless eye.
There buxom plenty never turns her horn;
The grace and virtue of exterior life,
No clean convenience reigns; even sleep itself

Least delicate of powers, reluctant there
Lays on the bed impure his heavy head.
Thy horrid walk! Dead, empty, unadorned,
See streets whose echoes never know the voice
Of cheerful hurry, commerce many-tongued,
And art mechanic at his various task
Fervent employed. Mark the desponding race,
Of occupation void, as void of hope;
Hope, the glad ray, glanced from Eternal Good,
That life enlivens, and exalts its powers,
With views of fortune-madness all to them!
By thee relentless seized their better joys,
To the soft aid of cordial airs they fly,
Breathing a kind oblivion o'er their woes,
And love and music melt their souls away.
From feeble Justice, see how rash Revenge,
Trembling, the balance snatches, and the sword,
Fearful himself, to venal ruffians gives.
See where God's altar, nursing murder, stands
With the red touch of dark assassins stained.

'But chief let Rome, the mighty city! speak
The full-exerted genius of thy reign.
Behold her rise amid the lifeless waste,
Expiring nature all corrupted round;
While the lone Tiber, through the desert plain,
Winds his waste stores, and sullen sweeps along.
Patched from my fragments, in unsolid pomp,
Mark how the temple glares; and, artful dressed,
Amusive draws the superstitious train.
Mark how the palace lifts a lying front,
Concealing often, in magnific jail,
Proud want; a deep unanimated gloom!
And oft adjoining to the drear abode
Of misery, whose melancholy walls
Seem its voracious grandeur to reproach.
Within the city bounds the desert see;
See the rank vine o'er subterranean roofs
Indecent spread; beneath whose fretted gold
It once exulting flowed. The people mark!
Matchless, while fired by me; to public good
Inexorably firm, just, generous, brave,
Afraid of nothing but unworthy life,
Elate with glory, an heroic soul
Known to the vulgar breast: behold them now
A thin despairing number, all-subdued,
The slaves of slaves, by superstition fooled,
By vice unmanned and a licentious rule,

In guile ingenious, and in murder brave.
Such in one land, beneath the same fair clime,
Thy sons, Oppression, are; and such were mine.

'Even with thy laboured pomp, for whose vain show
Deluded thousands starve—all age-begrimed,
Torn, robbed, and scattered in unnumbered sacks,
And by the tempest of two thousand years
Continual shaken, let my ruins vie—
These roads that yet the Roman hand assert,
Beyond the weak repair of modern toil;
These fractured arches, that the chiding stream
No more delighted hear; these rich remains
Of marbles now unknown, where shines imbibed
Each parent ray; these massy columns, hewed
From Afric's farthest shore; one granite all,
These obelisks high-towering to the sky,
Mysterious marked with dark Egyptian lore;
These endless wonders that this sacred way
Illumine still, and consecrate to fame;
These fountains, vases, urns, and statues, charged
With the fine stores of art-completing Greece.
Mine is, besides, thy every later boast—
Thy Buonarotis, thy Palladios mine;
And mine the fair designs which Raphael's soul,
O'er the live canvas emanating, breathed.

'What would you say, ye conquerors of earth!
Ye Romans! could you raise the laurelled head;
Could you the country see, by seas of blood
And the dread toil of ages won so dear,
Your pride, your triumph, your supreme delight!
For whose defence oft, in the doubtful hour,
You rush with rapture down the gulf of fate,
Of death ambitious! till by awful deeds,
Virtues, and courage that amaze mankind
The queen of nations rose; possessed of all
Which nature, art, and glory could bestow—
What would you say, deep in the last abyss
Of slavery, vice, and unambitious want,
Thus to behold her sunk? your crowded plains,
Void of their cities; unadorned your hills;
Ungraced your lakes; your ports to ships unknown;
Your lawless floods and your abandoned streams—
These could you know, these could you love again?
Thy Tibur, Horace, could it now inspire
Content, poetic ease, and rural joy
Soon bursting into song—while through the groves

Of headlong Anio, dashing to the vale
In many a tortured stream, you mused along?
Yon wild retreat, where superstition dreams,
Could, Tully, you your Tusculum believe?
And could you deem yon naked hills, that form,
Famed in old song, the ship-forsaken bay,
Your Formian shore? Once the delight of earth,
Where art and nature, ever smiling, joined
On the gay land to lavish all their stores—
How changed, how vacant, Virgil, wide around,
Would now your Naples seem? disastered less
By black Vesuvius thundering o'er the coast
His midnight earthquakes and his mining fires
Than by despotic rage, that inward gnaws,
A native foe—a foreign, tears without.
First from your flattered Caesars this began:
Till, doomed to tyrants an eternal prey,
Thin peopled spreads at last the syren plain,
That the dire soul of Hannibal disarmed;
And wrapped in weeds the shore of Venus lies.
There Baia sees no more the joyous throng,
Her banks all beaming with the pride of Rome;
No generous vines now bask along the hills,
Where sport the breezes of the Tyrrhene main;
With baths and temples mixed, no villas rise,
Nor, art—sustained amid reluctant waves,
Draw the cool murmurs of the breathing deep;
No spreading ports their sacred arms extend;
No mighty moles the big intrusive storm,
From the calm station, roll resounding back.
An almost total desolation sits,
A dreary stillness, saddening o'er the coast,
Where, when soft suns and tepid winters rose,
Rejoicing crowds inhaled the balm of peace,
Where citied hill to hill reflected blaze,
And where with Ceres Bacchus wont to hold
A genial strife. Her youthful form robust
Even nature yields, by fire and earthquake rent—
Whole stately cities in the dark abrupt
Swallowed at once, or vile in rubbish laid,
A nest for serpents; from the red abyss
New hills explosive thrown; the Lucrine lake
A reedy pool; and all to Cuma's point
The sea recovering his usurped domain,
And poured triumphant o'er the buried dome.

'Hence, Britain, learn—my best established, last,
And, more than Greece or Rome, my steady reign;

The land where, king and people equal bound
By guardian laws, my fullest blessings flow,
And where my jealous unsubmitting soul,
The dread of tyrants! burns in every breast—
Learn hence, if such the miserable fate
Of an heroic race, the masters once
Of humankind, what, when deprived of me,
How grievous must be thine? In spite of climes,
Whose sun-enlivened ether wakes the soul
To higher powers; in spite of happy soils,
That, but by labour's slightest aid impelled,
With treasures teem, to thy cold clime unknown;
If there desponding fail the common arts
And sustenance of life, could life itself,
Far less a thoughtless tyrant's hollow pomp,
Subsist with thee? Against depressing skies,
Joined to full-spread oppression's cloudy brow,
How could thy spirits hold? where vigour find
Forced fruits to tear from their unnative soil,
Or, storing every harvest in thy ports,
To plough the dreadful all-producing wave?'

Here paused the Goddess. By the pause assured,
In trembling accents thus I moved my prayer:

'Oh first, and most benevolent of powers!
Come from eternal splendours, here on earth,
Against despotic pride and rage and lust,
To shield mankind; to raise them to assert
The native rights and honour of their race—
Teach me, thy lowest subject, but in zeal
Yielding to none, the progress of thy reign,
And with a strain from thee enrich the muse.
As thee alone she serves, her patron, thou,
And great inspirer be! then will she joy,
Though narrow life her lot, and private shade:
And, when her venal voice she barters vile
Or to thy open or thy secret foes,
May ne'er those sacred raptures touch her more,
By slavish hearts unfelt! and may her song
Sink in oblivion with the nameless crew,
Vermin of state! to thy o'erflowing light
That owe their being, yet betray thy cause.'

Then, condescending kind, the heavenly Power
Returned:—'What here, suggested by the scene,
I slight unfold, record and sing at home,
In that blest isle, where (so we spirits move)

With one quick effort of my will I am.
There truth unlicensed walks; and dares accost
Even kings themselves, the monarchs of the free!
Fixed on my rock, there, an indulgent race
O'er Britons wield the sceptre of their choice;
And there, to finish what his sires began,
A Prince behold! for me who burns sincere,
Even with a subject's zeal. He my great work
Will parent-like sustain; and, added, give
The touch the graces and the muses owe.
For Britain's glory swells his panting breast,
And ancient arts he emulous revolves—
His pride to let the smiling heart abroad,
Through clouds of pomp, that but conceal the man;
To please his pleasure; bounty his delight;
And all the soul of Titus dwells in him.'

Hail, glorious theme! but how, alas! shall verse,
From the crude stores of mortal language drawn,
How faint and tedious, sing what, piercing deep,
The Goddess flashed at once upon my soul?
For, clear precision all, the tongue of gods
Is harmony itself; to every ear
Familiar known, like light to every eye.
Meantime disclosing ages, as she spoke,
In long succession poured their empires forth;
Scene after scene, the human drama spread;
And still the embodied picture rose to sight.

O thou! to whom the muses owe their flame;
Who bidd'st, beneath the pole, Parnassus rise,
And Hippocrene flow; with thy bold ease,
The striking force, the lightning of thy thought,
And thy strong phrase, that rolls profound and clear;
Oh, gracious Goddess! reinspire my song;
While I, to nobler than poetic fame
Aspiring, thy commands to Britons bear.

THE CONTENTS OF PART II

Liberty traced from the pastoral ages, and the first uniting of neighbouring families into civil government, to verse 46. The several establishments of Liberty, in Egypt, Persia, Phoenicia, Palestine, slightly touched upon, down to her great establishment in Greece, to verse 85. Geographical description of Greece, to verse 107. Sparta and Athens, the two principal states of Greece, described, to verse 158. Influence of Liberty over all the Grecian states; with regard to their government, their politeness, their virtues, their arts, and sciences. The vast superiority it gave them, in point of force and bravery, over the

Persians, exemplified by the action of Thermopylae, the battle of Marathon, and the retreat of the Ten Thousand. Its full exertion, and most beautiful effects in Athens, to verse 210. Liberty the source of free philosophy. The various schools which took their rise from Socrates, to verse 242. Enumeration of fine arts: Eloquence, Poetry, Music, Sculpture, Painting, and Architecture; the effects of Liberty in Greece, and brought to their utmost perfection there, to verse 392. Transition to the modern state of Greece, to verse 420. Why Liberty declined, and was at last entirely lost among the Greeks, to verse 481. Concluding Reflection.

PART II. GREECE

[First published in 1735]

Thus spoke the Goddess of the fearless eye,
And at her voice renewed the vision rose:
'First, in the dawn of time, with eastern swains
In woods, and tents, and cottages I lived;
While on from plain to plain they led their flocks
In search of clearer spring and fresher field.
These, as increasing families disclosed
The tender state, I taught an equal sway.
Few were offences, properties, and laws.
Beneath the rural portal, palm-o'erspread,
The father senate met. There justice dealt,
With reason then and equity the same,
Free as the common air her prompt decree;
Nor yet had stained her sword with subjects' blood.
The simpler arts were all their simple wants
Had urged to light. But instant, these supplied,
Another set of fonder wants arose,
And other arts with them of finer aim;
Till, from refining want to want impelled,
The mind by thinking pushed her latent powers,
And life began to glow and arts to shine.

'At first, on brutes alone the rustic war
Launched the rude spear; swift, as he glared along,
On the grim lion, or the robber wolf.
For then young sportive life was void of toil,
Demanding little, and with little pleased.
But, when to manhood grown, and endless joys,
Led on by equal toils, the bosom fired—
Lewd lazy rapine broke primeval peace,
And, hid in caves and idle forests drear,
From the lone pilgrim and the wandering swain
Seized what he durst not earn. Then brother's blood
First horrid smoked on the polluted skies.

Awful in justice, then the burning youth,
Led by their tempered sires, on lawless men,
The last worst monsters of the shaggy wood,
Turned the keen arrow, and the sharpened spear.
Then war grew glorious. Heroes then arose,
Who, scorning coward self, for others lived,
Toiled for their ease, and for their safety bled.
West with the living day to Greece I came:
Earth smiled beneath my beam: the muse before
Sonorous flew—that low till then in woods
Had tuned the reed, and sighed the shepherd's pain.
But now, to sing heroic deeds, she swelled
A nobler note, and bade the banquet burn.

'For Greece my sons of Egypt I forsook—
A boastful race! that in the vain abyss
Of fabling ages loved to lose their source,
And with their river traced it from the skies.
While there my laws alone despotic reigned,
And king, as well as people, proud obeyed.
I taught them science, virtue, wisdom, arts,
By poets, sages, legislators sought;
The school of polished life, and human kind.
But, when mysterious superstition came,
And, with her civil sister leagued, involved
In studied darkness the desponding mind—
Then tyrant power the righteous scourge unloosed:
For yielded reason speaks the soul a slave.
Instead of useful works, like nature's great,
Enormous cruel wonders crushed the land;
And round a tyrant's tomb, who none deserved,
For one vile carcass perished countless lives.
Then the great dragon couched amid his floods,
Swelled his fierce heart, and cried, "This flood is mine,
'Tis I that bid it flow." But, undeceived,
His frenzy soon the proud blasphemer felt;
Felt that, without my fertilizing power,
Suns lost their force, and Niles o'erflowed in vain.
Nought could retard me: nor the frugal state
Of rising Persia, sober in extreme
Beyond the pitch of man, and thence reversed
Into luxurious waste; nor yet the ports
Of old Phoenicia, first for letters famed,
That paint the voice, and silent speak to sight,
Of arts prime source, and guardian! by fair stars
First tempted out into the lonely deep,
To whom I first disclosed mechanic arts
The winds to conquer, to subdue the waves,

With all the peaceful power of ruling trade,
Earnest of Britain; nor by these retained,
Nor by the neighbouring land whose palmy shore
The silver Jordan laves. Before me lay
The promised land of arts, and urged my flight.

'Hail, nature's utmost boast! unrivalled Greece!
My fairest reign! where every power benign
Conspired to blow the flower of human kind,
And lavished all that genius can inspire.
Clear sunny climates, by the breezy main,
Ionian or Aegean, tempered kind:
Light, airy soils: a country rich and gay,
Broke into hills with balmy odours crowned,
And, bright with purple harvest, joyous vales:
Mountains and streams where verse spontaneous flowed,
Whence deemed by wondering men the seat of gods,
And still the mountains and the streams of song:
All that boon nature could luxuriant pour
Of high materials, and my restless arts
Frame into finished life. How many states,
And clustering towns, and monuments of fame,
And scenes of glorious deeds in little bounds!
From the rough tract of bending mountains, beat
By Adria's here, there by Aegean waves,
To where the deep-adorning Cyclad Isles
In shining prospect rise, and on the shore
Of farthest Crete resounds the Libyan main!

'O'er all two rival cities reared the brow,
And balanced all. Spread on Eurotas' bank,
Amid a circle of soft-rising hills,
The patient Sparta one: the sober, hard,
And man-subduing city, which no shape
Of pain could conquer, nor of pleasure charm.
Lycurgus there built, on the solid base
Of equal life, so well a tempered state,
Where mixed each government in such just poise,
Each power so checking and supporting each,
That firm for ages and unmoved it stood,
The fort of Greece! without one giddy hour,
One shock of faction or of party rage.
For, drained the springs of wealth, corruption there
Lay withered at the root. Thrice happy land!
Had not neglected art, with weedy vice
Confounded, sunk. But, if Athenian arts
Loved not the soil, yet there the calm abode
Of wisdom, virtue, philosophic ease,

Of manly sense and wit, in frugal phrase
Confined, and pressed into Laconic force.
There too, by rooting thence still treacherous self,
The public and the private grew the same.
The children of the nursing public all,
And at its table fed—for that they toiled,
For that they lived entire, and even for that
The tender mother urged her son to die.

'Of softer genius, but not less intense
To seize the palm of empire, Athens strove.
Where, with bright marbles big and future pomp,
Hymettus spread, amid the scented sky,
His thymy treasures to the labouring bee,
And to botanic hand the stores of health;
Wrapt in a soul-attenuating clime,
Between Ilissus and Cephissus glowed
This hive of science, shedding sweets divine
Of active arts and animated arms.
There, passionate for me, an easy-moved,
A quick, refined, a delicate, humane,
Enlightened people reigned. Oft on the brink
Of ruin, hurried by the charm of speech
Enforcing hasty counsel immature,
Tottered the rash democracy—unpoised,
And by the rage devoured that ever tears
A populace unequal, part too rich
And part or fierce with want or abject grown.
Solon at last, their mild restorer, rose,
Allayed the tempest, to the calm of laws
Reduced the settling whole, and, with the weight
Which the two senates to the public lent,
As with an anchor fixed the driving state.

'Nor was my forming care to these confined.
For emulation through the whole I poured,
Noble contention! who should most excel
In government well poised, adjusted best
To public weal; in countries cultured high;
In ornamented towns, where order reigns,
Free social life, and polished manners fair;
In exercise, and arms—arms only drawn
For common Greece to quell the Persian pride;
In moral science and in graceful arts.
Hence, as for glory peacefully they strove,
The prize grew greater, and the prize of all.
By contest brightened, hence the radiant youth
Poured every beam, by generous pride inflamed

Felt every ardour burn—their great reward
The verdant wreath which sounding Pisa gave.

'Hence flourished Greece; and hence a race of men,
As gods by conscious future times adored,
In whom each virtue wore a smiling air,
Each science shed o'er life a friendly light,
Each art was nature. Spartan valour hence,
At the famed pass, firm as an isthmus stood;
And the whole eastern ocean, waving far
As eye could dart its vision, nobly checked;
While in extended battle, at the field
Of Marathon, my keen Athenians drove
Before their ardent band an host of slaves.

'Hence through the continent ten thousand Greeks
Urged a retreat, whose glory not the prime
Of victories can reach. Deserts in vain
Opposed their course, and hostile lands unknown,
And deep rapacious floods, dire banked with death,
And mountains in whose jaws destruction grinned,
Hunger and toil, Armenian snows and storms,
And circling myriads still of barbarous foes.
Greece in their view, and glory yet untouched,
Their steady column pierced the scattering herds
Which a whole empire poured; and held its way
Triumphant, by the sage-exalted chief
Fired and sustained. Oh light and force of mind,
Almost almighty in severe extremes!
The sea at last from Colchian mountains seen,
Kind-hearted transport round their captains threw
The soldiers' fond embrace; o'erflowed their eyes
With tender floods, and loosed the general voice
To cries resounding loud—"The sea! the sea!"

'In Attic bounds hence heroes, sages, wits,
Shone thick as stars, the milky way of Greece!
And, though gay wit and pleasing grace was theirs,
All the soft modes of elegance and ease,
Yet was not courage less, the patient touch
Of toiling art, and disquisition deep.

'My spirit pours a vigour through the soul,
The unfettered thought with energy inspires,
Invincible in arts, in the bright field
Of nobler science as in that of arms.
Athenians thus not less intrepid burst
The bonds of tyrant darkness than they spurned

The Persian chains: while through the city, full
Of mirthful quarrel and of witty war,
Incessant struggled taste, refining taste,
And friendly free discussion, calling forth
From the fair jewel, truth, its latent ray.
O'er all shone out the great Athenian sage,
And father of philosophy—the sun,
From whose white blaze emerged each various sect
Took various tints, but with diminished beam.
Tutor of Athens! he in every street
Dealt priceless treasure—goodness his delight,
Wisdom his wealth, and glory his reward.
Deep through the human heart with playful art
His simple question stole, as into truth
And serious deeds he smiled the laughing race,
Taught moral happy life, whate'er can bless
Or grace mankind; and what he taught he was.
Compounded high, though plain, his doctrine broke
In different schools—the bold poetic phrase
Of figured Plato; Xenophon's pure strain,
Like the clear brook that steals along the vale;
Dissecting truth, the Stagyrite's keen eye;
The exalted Stoic pride; the Cynic sneer;
The slow-consenting Academic doubt;
And, joining bliss to virtue, the glad ease
Of Epicurus, seldom understood.
They, ever candid, reason still opposed
To reason; and, since virtue was their aim,
Each by sure practice tried to prove his way
The best. Then stood untouched the solid base
Of Liberty, the liberty of mind;
For systems yet, and soul-enslaving creeds,
Slept with the monsters of succeeding times.
From priestly darkness sprung the enlightening arts
Of fire, and sword, and rage, and horrid names.

'O Greece! thou sapient nurse of finer arts
Which to bright science blooming fancy bore!
Be this thy praise, that thou, and thou alone,
In these hast led the way, in these excelled,
Crowned with the laurel of assenting time.
'In thy full language, speaking mighty things,
Like a clear torrent close, or else diffused
A broad majestic stream, and rolling on
Through all the winding harmony of sound
In it the power of eloquence at large
Breathed the persuasive or pathetic soul,
Stilled by degrees the democratic storm,

Or bade it threatening rise, and tyrants shook
Flushed at the head of their victorious troops.
In it the muse, her fury never quenched
By mean unyielding phrase or jarring sound,
Her unconfined divinity displayed,
And still harmonious formed it to her will—
Or soft depressed it to the shepherd's moan
Or raised it swelling to the tongue of gods.

'Heroic song was thine; the fountain-bard,
Whence each poetic stream derives its course!
Thine the dread moral scene, thy chief delight!
Where idle fancy durst not mix her voice
When reason spoke august, the fervent heart
Or plained or stormed, and in the impassioned man,
Concealing art with art, the poet sunk.
This potent school of manners, but when left
To loose neglect a land-corrupting plague,
Was not unworthy deemed of public care
And boundless cost by thee—whose every son,
Even last mechanic, the true taste possessed
Of what had flavour to the nourished soul.
'The sweet enforcer of the poet's strain,
Thine was the meaning music of the heart.
Not the vain trill, that, void of passion, runs
In giddy mazes, tickling idle ears;
But that deep-searching voice, and artful hand,
To which respondent shakes the varied soul.

'Thy fair ideas, thy delightful forms,
By love imagined, and the graces touched,
The boast of well pleased nature! Sculpture seized,
And bade them ever smile in Parian stone.
Selecting beauty's choice, and that again
Exalting, blending in a perfect whole,
Thy workmen left even nature's self behind.
From those far different whose prolific hand
Peoples a nation, they for years on years,
By the cool touches of judicious toil,
Their rapid genius curbing, poured it all
Through the live features of one breathing stone.
There, beaming full, it shone, expressing gods—
Jove's awful brow, Apollo's air divine,
The fierce atrocious frown of sinewed Mars,
Or the sly graces of the Cyprian queen.
Minutely perfect all! Each dimple sunk,
And every muscle swelled, as nature taught.
In tresses, braided gay, the marble waved;

Flowed in loose robes, or thin transparent veils;
Sprung into motion; softened into flesh;
Was fired to passion, or refined to soul.

'Nor less thy pencil with creative touch
Shed mimic life, when all thy brightest dames
Assembled Zeuxis in his Helen mixed;
And when Apelles, who peculiar knew
To give a grace that more than mortal smiled,
The soul of beauty! called the queen of love
Fresh from the billows blushing orient charms.
Even such enchantment then thy pencil poured
That cruel-thoughted war the impatient torch
Dashed to the ground, and, rather than destroy
The patriot picture, let the city 'scape.

'First, elder Sculpture taught her sister art
Correct design; where great ideas shone,
And in the secret trace expression spoke;
Taught her the graceful attitude, the turn
And beauteous airs of head; the native act,
Or bold or easy; and, cast free behind,
The swelling mantle's well adjusted flow.
Then the bright muse, their eldest sister, came,
And bade her follow where she led the way—
Bade earth, and sea, and air in colours rise,
And copious action on the canvas glow:
Gave her gay fable; spread invention's store;
Enlarged her view; taught composition high,
And just arrangement, circling round one point
That starts to sight, binds and commands the whole.
Caught from the heavenly muse a nobler aim,
And scorning the soft trade of mere delight,
O'er all thy temples, porticos, and schools,
Heroic deeds she traced, and warm displayed
Each moral beauty to the ravished eye.
There, as the imagined presence of the god
Aroused the mind, or vacant hours induced
Calm contemplation, or assembled youth
Burned in ambitious circle round the sage,
The living lesson stole into the heart
With more prevailing force than dwells in words.
These rouse to glory; while to rural life
The softer canvas oft reposed the soul.
There gaily broke the sun-illumined cloud;
The lessening prospect, and the mountain blue
Vanished in air; the precipice frowned dire;
White down the rock the rushing torrent dashed;

The sun shone trembling o'er the distant main;
The tempest foamed immense; the driving storm
Saddened the skies, and, from the doubling gloom,
On the scathed oak the ragged lightning fell;
In closing shades, and where the current strays,
With peace and love and innocence around,
Piped the lone shepherd to his feeding flock;
Round happy parents smiled their younger selves;
And friends conversed, by death divided long.

'To public virtue thus the smiling arts,
Unblemished handmaids, served; the graces they
To dress this fairest Venus. Thus revered,
And placed beyond the reach of sordid care,
The high awarders of immortal fame,
Alone for glory thy great masters strove;
Courted by kings, and by contending states
Assumed the boasted honour of their birth.

'In architecture too thy rank supreme!
That art where most magnificent appears
The little builder man; by thee refined,
And, smiling high, to full perfection brought.
Such thy sure rules that Goths of every age,
Who scorned their aid, have only loaded earth
With laboured heavy monuments of shame.
Not those gay domes that o'er thy splendid shore
Shot, all proportion, up. First, unadorned
And nobly plain, the manly Doric rose;
The Ionic then, with decent matron grace,
Her airy pillar heaved; luxuriant, last,
The rich Corinthian spread her wanton wreath.
The whole so measured true, so lessened off
By fine proportion, that the marble pile,
Formed to repel the still or stormy waste
Of rolling ages, light as fabrics looked
That from the magic wand aerial rise.

'These were the wonders that illumined Greece,
From end to end—' Here interrupting warm,
'Where are they now? (I cried) say, goddess, where?
And what the land, thy darling thus of old?'

'Sunk!' (she resumed), 'deep in the kindred gloom
Of superstition and of slavery sunk!
No glory now can touch their hearts, benumbed
By loose dejected sloth and servile fear;
No science pierce the darkness of their minds;

No nobler art the quick ambitious soul
Of imitation in their breast awake.
Even to supply the needful arts of life
Mechanic toil denies the hopeless hand.
Scarce any trace remaining, vestige grey,
Or nodding column on the desert shore
To point where Corinth or where Athens stood.
A faithless land of violence, and death!
Where commerce parleys dubious on the shore;
And his wild impulse curious search restrains,
Afraid to trust the inhospitable clime.
Neglected nature fails; in sordid want
Sunk and debased, their beauty beams no more.
The sun himself seems, angry, to regard
Of light unworthy the degenerate race,
And fires them oft with pestilential rays—
While earth, blue poison steaming on the skies,
Indignant shakes them from her troubled sides.
But as from man to man, fate's first decree,
Impartial death the tide of riches rolls,
So states must die and Liberty go round.

'Fierce was the stand ere virtue, valour, arts,
And the soul fired by me (that often, stung
With thoughts of better times and old renown,
From hydra-tyrants tried to clear the land)
Lay quite extinct in Greece, their works effaced,
And gross o'er all unfeeling bondage spread.
Sooner I moved my much reluctant flight,
Poised on the doubtful wing, when Greece with Greece,
Embroiled in foul contention, fought no more
For common glory and for common weal,
But, false to Freedom, sought to quell the free;
Broke the firm band of peace and sacred love,
That lent the whole irrefragable force,
And, as around the partial trophy blushed,
Prepared the way for total overthrow.
Then to the Persian power, whose pride they scorned,
When Xerxes poured his millions o'er the land,
Sparta, by turns, and Athens vilely sued;
Sued to be venal parricides, to spill
Their country's bravest blood, and on themselves
To turn their matchless mercenary arms.
Peaceful in Susa, then, sat the great king;
And by the trick of treaties, the still waste
Of sly corruption and barbaric gold,
Effected what his steel could ne'er perform.
Profuse he gave them the luxurious draught,

Inflaming all the land-unbalanced wide
Their tottering states; their wild assemblies ruled,
As the winds turn at every blast the seas—
And by their listed orators, whose breath
Still with a factious storm infested Greece,
Roused them to civil war, or dashed them down
To sordid peace—peace! that, when Sparta shook
Astonished Artaxerxes on his throne,
Gave up, fair-spread o'er Asia's sunny shore,
Their kindred cities to perpetual chains.

'What could so base, so infamous a thought
In Spartan hearts inspire? Jealous they saw
Respiring Athens rear again her walls:
And the pale fury fired them once again
To crush this rival city to the dust.
For now no more the noble social soul
Of Liberty my families combined;
But by short views and selfish passions broke,
Dire as when friends are rankled into foes
They mixed severe, and waged eternal war:
Nor felt they furious their exhausted force;
Nor, with false glory, discord, madness blind,
Saw how the blackening storm from Thracia came.
Long years rolled on, by many a battle stained,
The blush and boast of fame! where courage, art,
And military glory shone supreme:
But let detesting ages from the scene
Of Greece self-mangled turn the sickening eye.
At last, when bleeding from a thousand wounds
She felt her spirits fail, and in the dust
Her latest heroes, Nicias, Conon, lay,
Agesilaus, and the Theban friends—
The Macedonian vulture marked his time,
By the dire scent of Cheronaea lured,
And, fierce descending, seized his hapless prey.

'Thus tame submitted to the victor's yoke
Greece, once the gay, the turbulent, the bold;
For every grace, and muse, and science born;
With arts of war, of government elate;
To tyrants dreadful, dreadful to the best;
Whom I myself could scarcely rule: and thus
The Persian fetters, that enthralled the mind,
Were turned to formal and apparent chains.

'Unless corruption first deject the pride
And guardian vigour of the free-born soul,

All crude attempts of violence are vain;
For, firm within, and while at heart untouched,
Ne'er yet by force was freedom overcome.
But, soon as Independence stoops the head,
To vice enslaved and vice-created wants,
Then to some foul corrupting hand, whose waste
These heightened wants with fatal bounty feeds—
From man to man the slackening ruin runs,
Till the whole state unnerved in slavery sinks.'

THE CONTENTS OF PART III

As this part contains a description of the establishment of Liberty in Rome, it begins with a view of the Grecian Colonies settled in the southern parts of Italy, which with Sicily constituted the Great Greece of the Ancients. With these colonies the Spirit of Liberty and of Republics spreads over Italy, to verse 31. Transition to Pythagoras and his philosophy, which he taught through these free states and cities, to verse 70. Amidst the many small Republics in Italy, Rome the destined seat of Liberty. Her establishment there dated from the expulsion of the Tarquins. How differing from that in Greece, to verse 87.

Reference to a view of the Roman Republic given in the first part of this Poem: to mark its rise and fall the peculiar purport of this. During its first ages, the greatest force of Liberty and Virtue exerted, to verse 102. The source whence derived the Heroic Virtues of the Romans. Enumeration, of these Virtues. Thence their security at home; their glory, sl1ccess, and empire abroad, to verse 225. Bounds of the Roman empire geographically described, to verse 256. The states of Greece restored to Liberty by Titus Quintus Flaminius, the highest instance of public generosity and beneficence, to verse 327. The loss of Liberty in Rome, to verse 360. Its causes, progress, and completion in the death of Brutus, to verse 483. Rome under the emperors, to verse 511. From Rome the Goddess of Liberty goes among the Northern Nations; where, by infusing into them her Spirit and general principles, she lays the groundwork of her future establishments; sends them in vengeance on the Roman Empire, now totally enslaved; and then, with Arts and Sciences in her train, quits Earth during the dark ages, to verse 548. The celestial regions, to which Liberty retired, not proper to be opened to the view of mortals.

PART III. ROME

[First published in the end of 1735]

Here melting mixed with air the ideal forms
That painted still whate'er the goddess sung.
Then I, impatient:—'From extinguished Greece,
To what new region streamed the human day?'

She softly sighing, as when Zephyr leaves,
Resigned to Boreas, the declining year,
Resumed:—'Indignant, these last scenes I fled;

And long ere then, Leucadia's cloudy cliff
And the Ceraunian hills behind me thrown,
All Latium stood aroused. Ages before,
Great mother of republics! Greece had poured,
Swarm after swarm, her ardent youth around.
On Asia, Afric, Sicily, they stooped,
But chief on fair Hesperia's winding shore;
Where, from Lacinium to Etrurian vales,
They rolled increasing colonies along,
And lent materials for my Roman reign.
With them my spirit spread; and numerous states
And cities rose on Grecian models formed,
As its parental policy and arts
Each had imbibed. Besides, to each assigned,
A guardian genius o'er the public weal
Kept an unclosing eye; tried to sustain
Or more sublime the soul infused by me:
And strong the battle rose, with various wave,
Against the tyrant demons of the land.
Thus they their little wars and triumphs knew,
Their flows of fortune and receding times—
But almost all below the proud regard
Of story vowed to Rome, on deeds intent
That truth beyond the flight of fable bore.

'Not so the Samian sage; to him belongs
The brightest witness of recording fame.
For these free states his native isle forsook
And a vain tyrant's transitory smile,
He sought Crotona's pure salubrious air,
And through Great Greece his gentle wisdom taught—
Wisdom that calmed for listening years the mind,
Nor ever heard amid the storm of zeal.
His mental eye first launched into the deeps
Of boundless ether, where unnumbered orbs,
Myriads on myriads, through the pathless sky
Unerring roll, and wind their steady way.
There he the full consenting choir beheld;
There first discerned the secret band of love,
The kind attraction that to central suns
Binds circling earths, and world with world unites.
Instructed thence, he great ideas formed
Of the whole—moving, all-informing God,
The Sun of beings! beaming unconfined
Light, life, and love, and ever active power—
Whom nought can image, and who best approves
The silent worship of the moral heart,
That joys in bounteous Heaven and spreads the joy.

Nor scorned the soaring sage to stoop to life,
And bound his reason to the sphere of man.
He gave the four yet reigning virtues name,
Inspired the study of the finer arts,
That civilize mankind, and laws devised
Where with enlightened justice mercy mixed.
He even into his tender system took
Whatever shares the brotherhood of life:
He taught that life's indissoluble flame,
From brute to man, and man to brute again,
For ever shifting, runs the eternal round;
Thence tried against the blood-polluted meal,
And limbs yet quivering with some kindred soul,
To turn the human heart. Delightful truth!
Had he beheld the living chain ascend,
And not a circling form, but rising whole.

'Amid these small republics one arose
On yellow Tiber's bank, almighty Rome,
Fated for me. A nobler spirit warmed
Her sons; and, roused by tyrants, nobler still
It burned in Brutus, the proud Tarquins chased
With all their crimes, bade radiant eras rise
And the long honours of the consul line.

'Here from the fairer, not the greater, plan
Of Greece I varied; whose unmixing states,
By the keen soul of emulation pierced,
Long waged alone the bloodless war of arts,
And their best empire gained. But to diffuse
O'er men an empire was my purpose now—
To let my martial majesty abroad;
Into the vortex of one state to draw
The whole mixed force, and liberty, on earth;
To conquer tyrants, and set nations free.

'Already have I given, with flying touch,
A broken view of this my amplest reign.
Now, while its first, last, periods you survey, go
Mark how it labouring rose, and rapid fell.

'When Rome in noon-tide empire grasped the world,
And, soon as her resistless legions shone,
The nations stooped around, though then appeared
Her grandeur most, yet in her dawn of power,
By many a jealous equal people pressed,
Then was the toil, the mighty struggle then.
Then for each Roman I an hero told;

And every passing sun and Latian scene
Saw patriot virtues then and awful deeds
That or surpass the faith of modern times
Or, if believed, with sacred horror strike.

'For then, to prove my most exalted power,
I to the point of full perfection pushed,
To fondness and enthusiastic zeal,
The great, the reigning passion of the free.
That godlike passion! which, the bounds of self
Divinely bursting, the whole public takes
Into the heart, enlarged, and burning high
With the mixed ardour of unnumbered selves—
Of all who safe beneath the voted laws
Of the same parent state fraternal live.
From this kind sun of moral nature flowed
Virtues that shine the light of humankind,
And, rayed through story, warm remotest time.
These virtues too, reflected to their source,
Increased its flame. The social charm went round,
The fair idea, more attractive still
As more by virtue marked; till Romans, all
One band of friends, unconquerable grew.

'Hence, when their country raised her plaintive voice,
The voice of pleading nature was not heard;
And in their hearts the fathers throbbed no more—
Stern to themselves, but gentle to the whole.
Hence sweetened pain, the luxury of toil;
Patience, that baffled fortune's utmost rage;
High-minded hope, which at the lowest ebb,
When Brennus conquered and when Cannae bled,
The bravest impulse felt and scorned despair.
Hence moderation a new conquest gained—
As on the vanquished, like descending heaven,
Their dewy mercy dropped, their bounty beamed,
And by the labouring hand were crowns bestowed.
Fruitful of men, hence hard laborious life,
Which no fatigue can quell, no season pierce.
Hence Independence, with his little pleased,
Serene and self-sufficient like a god,
In whom corruption could not lodge one charm;
While he his honest roots to gold preferred;
While truly rich, and by his Sabine field
The man maintained, the Roman's splendour all
Was in the public wealth and glory placed—
Or ready, a rough swain, to guide the plough,
Or else, the purple o'er his shoulder thrown

In long majestic flow, to rule the state
With wisdom's purest eye, or, clad in steel,
To drive the steady battle on the foe.
Hence every passion, even the proudest, stooped
To common good—Camillus, thy revenge;
Thy glory, Fabius. All submissive hence,
Consuls, dictators, still resigned their rule,
The very moment that the laws ordained.
Though conquest o'er them clapped her eagle wings,
Her laurels wreathed, and yoked her snowy steeds
To the triumphal car—soon as expired
The latest hour of sway, taught to submit
(A harder lesson that than to command),
Into the private Roman sunk the Chief.
If Rome was served and glorious, careless they
By whom. Their country's fame they deemed their own,
And, above envy, in a rival's train
Sung the loud Ios by themselves deserved.
Hence matchless courage. On Cremera's bank,
Hence fell the Fabii; hence the Decii died;
And Curtius plunged into the flaming gulf.
Hence Regulus the wavering fathers firmed
By dreadful counsel never given before,
For Roman honour sued, and his own doom.
Hence he sustained to dare a death prepared
By Punic rage. On earth his manly look
Relentless fixed, he from a last embrace,
By chains polluted, put his wife aside,
His little children climbing for a kiss;
Then dumb through rows of weeping, wondering friends,
A new illustrious exile! pressed along.
Nor less impatient did he pierce the crowds
Opposing his return, than if, escaped
From long litigious suits, he glad forsook
The noisy town a while and city cloud
To breathe Venafrian or Tarentine air.
Need I these high particulars recount?
The meanest bosom felt a thirst for fame;
Flight their worst death, and shame their only fear.
Life had no charms, nor any terrors fate,
When Rome and glory called. But, in one view,
Mark the rare boast of these unequalled times.
Ages revolved unsullied by a crime:
Astrea reigned, and scarcely needed laws
To bind a race elated with the pride
Of virtue, and disdaining to descend
To meanness, mutual violence, and wrongs.
While war around them raged, in happy Rome

All peaceful smiled, all save the passing clouds
That often hang on Freedom's jealous brow;
And fair unblemished centuries elapsed
When not a Roman bled but in the field.
Their virtue such that an unbalanced state,
Still between noble and plebeian tossed,
As flowed the wave of fluctuating power,
By that kept firm and with triumphant prow
Rode out the storms. Oft though the native feuds
That from the first their constitution shook
(A latent ruin, growing as it grew)
Stood on the threatening point of civil war
Ready to rush—yet could the lenient voice
Of wisdom, soothing the tumultuous soul,
These sons of virtue calm. Their generous hearts,
Unpetrified by self, so naked lay
And sensible to truth that o'er the rage
Of giddy faction, by oppression swelled,
Prevailed a simple fable, and at once
To peace recovered the divided state.
But, if their often-cheated hopes refused
The soothing touch, still, in the love of Rome,
The dread dictator found a sure resource.
Was she assaulted? was her glory stained?
One common quarrel wide inflamed the whole.
Foes in the forum in the field were friends,
By social danger bound—each fond for each,
And for their dearest country all, to die.

'Thus up the hill of empire slow they toiled,
Till, the bold summit gained, the thousand states
Of proud Italia blended into one;
Then o'er the nations they resistless rushed,
And touched the limits of the failing world.

'Let fancy's eye the distant lines unite.
See that which borders wild the western main,
Where storms at large resound, and tides immense;
From Caledonia's dim cerulean coast,
And moist Hibernia, to where Atlas, lodged
Amid the restless clouds and leaning heaven,
Hangs o'er the deep that borrows thence its name.
Mark that opposed, where first the springing morn
Her roses sheds, and shakes around her dews—
From the dire deserts by the Caspian laved
To where the Tigris and Euphrates, joined,
Impetuous tear the Babylonian plain,
And blest Arabia aromatic breathes.

See that dividing far the watery north,
Parent of floods! from the majestic Rhine,
Drunk by Batavian meads, to where, seven-mouthed,
In Euxine waves the flashing Danube roars;
To where the frozen Tanais scarcely stirs
The dead Maeotic pool, or the long Rha
In the black Scythian sea his torrent throws.
Last, that beneath the burning zone behold.
See where it runs from the deep-loaded plains
Of Mauritania to the Libyan sands,
Where Ammon lifts amid the torrid waste
A verdant isle with shade and fountain fresh,
And farther to the full Egyptian shore,
To where the Nile from Ethiopian clouds,
His never drained ethereal urn, descends.
In this vast space what various tongues and states!
What bounding rocks and mountains, floods and seas!
What purple tyrants quelled, and nations freed!

'O'er Greece descended chief, with stealth divine,
The Roman bounty in a flood of day:
As at her Isthmian games, a fading pomp!
Her full-assembled youth innumerous swarmed.
On a tribunal raised Flaminius sat:
A victor he, from the deep phalanx pierced
Of iron-coated Macedon, and back
The Grecian tyrant to his bounds repelled.
In the high thoughtless gaiety of game,
While sport alone their unambitious hearts
Possessed, the sudden trumpet, sounding hoarse,
Bade silence o'er the bright assembly reign.
Then thus a herald:—"To the states of Greece
The Roman people unconfined restore
Their countries, cities, liberties, and laws:
Taxes remit, and garrisons withdraw."
The crowd, astonished half, and half informed,
Stared dubious round; some questioned, some exclaimed
(Like one who dreaming, between hope and fear,
Is lost in anxious joy)—"Be that again,
Be that again proclaimed, distinct and loud."
Loud and distinct it was again proclaimed;
And, still as midnight in the rural shade
When the gale slumbers, they the words devoured.
A while severe amazement held them mute,
Then, bursting broad, the boundless shout to heaven
From many a thousand hearts ecstatic sprung.
On every hand rebellowed to their joy
The swelling sea, the rocks and vocal hills:

Through all her turrets stately Corinth shook;
And, from the void above of shattered air,
The flitting bird fell breathless to the ground.
What piercing bliss, how keen a sense of fame
Did then, Flaminius, reach thy inmost soul!
And with what deep-felt glory didst thou then
Escape the fondness of transported Greece!
Mixed in a tempest of superior joy,
They left the sports; like Bacchanals they flew,
Each other straining in a strict embrace,
Nor strained a slave; and loud acclaims till night
Round the Proconsul's tent repeated rung.
Then, crowned with garlands, came the festive hours;
And music, sparkling wine, and converse warm
Their raptures waked anew. "Ye gods!" they cried,
"Ye guardian gods of Greece! and are we free?
Was it not madness deemed the very thought?
And is it true? How did we purchase chains?
At what a dire expense of kindred blood?
And are they now dissolved? And scarce one drop
For the fair first of blessings have we paid?
Courage and conduct in the doubtful field
When rages wide the storm of mingling war
Are rare indeed; but how to generous ends
To turn success and conquest, rarer still
That the great gods and Romans only know.
Lives there on earth, almost to Greece unknown,
A people so magnanimous to quit
Their native soil, traverse the stormy deep,
And by their blood and treasure, spent for us,
Redeem our states, our liberties, and laws!
There does! there does! Oh Saviour Titus! Rome!"
Thus through the happy night they poured their souls,
And in my last reflected beams rejoiced.
As when the shepherd, on the mountain brow,
Sits piping to his flocks and gamesome kids;
Meantime the sun, beneath the green earth sunk,
Slants upward o'er the scene a parting gleam:
Short is the glory that the mountain gilds,
Plays on the glittering flocks and glads the swain
To western worlds irrevocable rolled,
Rapid the source of light recalls his ray.'

Here interposing I:—'Oh, Queen of men!
Beneath whose sceptre in essential rights
Equal they live, though placed for common good
Various, or in subjection or command,
And that by common choice—alas! the scene,

With virtue, freedom, and with glory bright,
Streams into blood and darkens into woe.'

Thus she pursued:—'Near this great era, Rome
Began to feel the swift approach of fate,
That now her vitals gained—still more and more
Her deep divisions kindling into rage
And war, with chains and desolation charged.
From an unequal balance of her sons
These fierce contentions sprung: and, as increased
This hated inequality, more fierce
They flamed to tumult. Independence failed
Here by luxurious wants, by real there;
And with this virtue every virtue sunk
As, with the sliding rock, the pile sustained.
A last attempt, too late, the Gracchi made
To fix the flying scale and poise the state.
On one side swelled aristocratic Pride,
With Usury, the villain! whose fell gripe
Bends by degrees to baseness the free soul,
And Luxury rapacious, cruel, mean,
Mother of vice! While on the other crept
A populace in want, with pleasure fired;
Fit for proscriptions, for the darkest deeds,
As the proud feeder bade; inconstant, blind,
Deserting friends at need, and duped by foes;
Loud and seditious, when a chief inspired
Their headlong fury, but, of him deprived,
Already slaves that licked the scourging hand.

'This firm republic that against the blast
Of opposition rose, that (like an oak,
Nursed on feracious Algidum, whose boughs
Still stronger shoot beneath the rigid axe)
By loss, by slaughter, from the steel itself
Even force and spirit drew, smit with the calm,
The dead serene of prosperous fortune, pined.
Nought now her weighty legions could oppose;
Her terror, once, on Afric's tawny shore
Now smoked in dust, a stabling now for wolves;
And every dreaded power received the yoke.
Besides, destructive, from the conquered east
In the soft plunder came that worst of plagues,
The pestilence of mind, a fevered thirst
For the false joys which luxury prepares.
Unworthy joys! that wasteful leave behind
No mark of honour in reflecting hour,
No secret ray to glad the conscious soul

At once involving in one ruin wealth
And wealth-acquiring powers, while stupid self,
Of narrow gust, and hebetating sense
Devour the nobler faculties of bliss.
Hence Roman virtue slackened into sloth,
Security relaxed the softening state,
And the broad eye of government lay closed.
No more the laws inviolable reigned,
And public weal no more: but party raged,
And partial power and licence uurestrained
Let discord through the deathful city loose.
First, mild Tiberius, on thy sacred head
The fury's vengeance fell; the first whose blood
Had, since the consuls, stained contending Rome.
Of precedent pernicious! with thee bled
Three hundred Romans; with thy brother, next,
Three thousand more—till, into battles turned
Debates of peace, and forced the trembling laws,
The forum and comitia horrid grew,
A scene of bartered power or reeking gore.
When, half-ashamed, corruption's thievish arts
And ruffian force begin to sap the mounds
And majesty of laws; if not in time
Repressed severe, for human aid too strong
The torrent turns, and overbears the whole.

'Thus luxury, dissension, a mixed rage
Of boundless pleasure and of boundless wealth,
Want wishing change, and waste-repairing war,
Rapine for ever lost to peaceful toil,
Guilt unatoned, profuse of blood revenge,
Corruption all avowed, and lawless force,
Each heightening each, alternate shook the state.
Meantime ambition, at the dazzling head
Of hardy legions, with the laurels heaped
And spoil of nations, in one circling blast
Combined in various storm, and from its base
The broad republic tore. By virtue built
It touched the skies, and spread o'er sheltered earth
An ample roof: by virtue too sustained,
And balanced steady, every tempest sung
Innoxious by, or bade it firmer stand.
But when, with sudden and enormous change,
The first of mankind sunk into the last,
As once in virtue, so in vice extreme,
This universal fabric yielded loose,
Before ambition still; and thundering down,
At last, beneath its ruins crushed a world.

A conquering people to themselves a prey
Must ever fall, when their victorious troops,
In blood and rapine savage grown, can find
No land to sack and pillage but their own.

'By brutal Marius, and keen Sylla, first
Effused the deluge dire of civil blood,
Unceasing woes began, and this, or that,
(Deep-drenching their revenge) nor virtue spared,
Nor sex, nor age, nor quality, nor name;
Till Rome, into an human shambles turned,
Made deserts lovely.—Oh, to well-earned chains,
Devoted race!—If no true Roman then,
No Scaevola, there was to raise for me
A vengeful hand—was there no father, robbed
Of blooming youth to prop his withered age?
No son, a witness to his hoary sire
In dust and gore defiled? no friend, forlorn?
No wretch that doubtful trembled for himself?
None brave, or wild, to pierce a monster's heart,
Who, heaping horror round, no more deserved
The sacred shelter of the laws he spurned?
No:—Sad o'er all profound dejection sat;
And nerveless fear. The slave's asylum theirs—
Or flight, ill-judging that the timid back
Turns weak to slaughter, or partaken guilt.
In vain from Sylla's vanity I drew
An unexampled deed. The power resigned,
And all unhoped the commonwealth restored,
Amazed the public, and effaced his crimes.
Through streets yet streaming from his murderous hand
Unarmed he strayed, unguarded, unassailed,
And on the bed of peace his ashes laid—
A grace, which I to his demission gave.
But with him died not the despotic soul.
Ambition saw that stooping Rome could bear
A master, nor had virtue to be free.
Hence, for succeeding years, my troubled reign
No certain peace, no spreading prospect knew.
Destruction gathered round. Still the black soul
Or of a Catiline or Rullus swelled
With fell designs; and all the watchful art
Of Cicero demanded, all the force,
All the state-wielding magic of his tongue,
And all the thunder of my Cato's zeal.
With these I lingered; till the flame anew
Burst out in blaze immense, and wrapped the world.
The shameful contest sprung; to whom mankind

Should yield the neck—to Pompey, who concealed
A rage impatient of an equal name,
Or to the nobler Caesar, on whose brow
O'er daring vice deluding virtue smiled,
And who no less a vain superior scorned.
Both bled, but bled in vain. New traitors rose.
The venal will be bought, the base have lords.
To these vile wars I left ambitious slaves;
And from Philippi's field, from where in dust
The last of Romans, matchless Brutus! lay,
Spread to the north untamed a rapid wing.

'What though the first smooth Caesars arts caressed,
Merit, and virtue, simulating me?
Severely tender, cruelly humane
The chain to clinch, and make it softer sit
On the new-broken still ferocious state!
From the dark third, succeeding, I beheld
The imperial monsters all—a race on earth
Vindictive sent, the scourge of humankind!
Whose blind profusion drained a bankrupt world;
Whose lust to forming nature seems disgrace;
And whose infernal rage bade every drop
Of ancient blood that yet retained my flame,
To that of Paetus, in the peaceful bath
Or Rome's affrighted streets inglorious flow.
But almost just the meanly patient death
That waits a tyrant's unprevented stroke.
Titus indeed gave one short evening gleam;
More cordial felt, as in the midst it spread
Of storm and horror. The delight of men!
He who the day when his o'erflowing hand
Had made no happy heart concluded lost;
Trajan and he, with the mild sire and son,
His son of virtue! eased awhile mankind;
And arts revived beneath their gentle beam.
Then was their last effort: what sculpture raised
To Trajan's glory following triumphs stole,
And mixed with Gothic forms (the chisel's shame)
On that triumphal arch the forms of Greece.

'Meantime o'er rocky Thrace and the deep vales
Of gelid Haemus I pursued my flight;
And, piercing farthest Scythia, westward swept
Sarmatia, traversed by a thousand streams,
A sullen land of lakes, and fens immense,
Of rocks, resounding torrents, gloomy heaths,
And cruel deserts black with sounding pine,

Where nature frowns—though sometimes into smiles
She softens, and immediate at the touch
Of southern gales throws from the sudden glebe
Luxuriant pasture and a waste of flowers.
But, cold-compressed, when the whole-loaded heaven
Descends in snow, lost in one white abrupt
Lies undistinguished Earth; and, seized by frost,
Lakes, headlong streams, and floods, and oceans sleep.
Yet there life glows; the furry millions there
Deep-dig their dens beneath the sheltering snows:
And there a race of men prolific swarms,
To various pain, to little pleasure used,
On whom keen-parching beat Riphaean winds,
Hard like their soil, and like their climate fierce,
The nursery of nations!—These I roused,
Drove land on land, on people people poured,
Till from almost perpetual night they broke
As if in search of day, and o'er the banks
Of yielding empire, only slave-sustained,
Resistless raged—in vengeance urged by me.

'Long in the barbarous heart the buried seeds
Of freedom lay, for many a wintry age;
And, though my spirit worked, by slow degrees
Nought but its pride and fierceness yet appeared.
Then was the night of time, that parted worlds.
I quitted earth the while. As when the tribes
Aerial, warned of rising winter, ride
Autumnal winds, to warmer climates borne—
So, arts and each good genius in my train,
I cut the closing gloom, and soared to heaven.

'In the bright regions there of purest day,
Far other scenes and palaces arise,
Adorned profuse with other arts divine.
All beauty here below, to them compared,
Would, like a rose before the midday sun,
Shrink up its blossom—like a bubble break
The passing poor magnificence of kings.
For there the king of nature in full blaze
Calls every splendour forth, and there his court,
Amid ethereal powers and virtues holds—
Angel, archangel, tutelary gods,
Of cities, nations, empires, and of worlds.
But sacred be the veil that kindly clouds
A light too keen for mortals—wraps a view
Too softening fair, for those that here in dust
Must cheerful toil out their appointed years.

A sense of higher life would only damp
The schoolboy's task, and spoil his playful hours.
Nor could the child of reason, feeble man,
With vigour through this infant-being drudge,
Did brighter worlds, their unimagined bliss
Disclosing, dazzle and dissolve his mind.'

THE CONTENTS OF PART IV

Difference betwixt the Ancients and Moderns slightly touched upon, to verse 29. Description of the Dark Ages. The Goddess of Liberty, who during these is supposed to have left earth, returns, attended with Arts and Science, to verse 99. She first descends on Italy. Sculpture, Painting, and Architecture fix at Rome, to revive their several arts by the great models of antiquity there, which many barbarous invasions had not been able to destroy. The revival of these arts marked out. That sometimes arts may flourish for a while under despotic governments, though never the natural and genuine production of them, to verse 253. Learning begins to dawn. The Muse and Science attend Liberty, who in her progress towards Great Britain raises several free states and cities. These enumerated, to verse 380. Author's exclamation of joy, upon seeing the British seas and coasts rise in the Vision, which painted whatever the Goddess of Liberty said. She resumes her narration, the Genius of the Deep appears, and addressing Liberty, associates Great Britain into his dominion, to verse 450. Liberty received and congratulated by Britannia, and the native Genii or Virtues of the island. These described. Animated by the presence of Liberty, they begin their operations. Their beneficent influence contrasted with the works and delusions of opposing Demons, to verse 623. Concludes with an abstract of the English history, marking the several advances of Liberty, down to her complete establishment at the Revolution.

PART IV. BRITAIN

[First published, 1736]

Struck with the rising scene, thus I amazed:—
'Ah, Goddess, what a change! is Earth the same?
Of the same kind the ruthless race she feeds?
And does the same fair sun and ether spread
Round this vile spot their all-enlivening soul?
Lo! beauty fails; lost in unlovely forms
Of little pomp, magnificence no more
Exalts the mind, and bids the public smile—
While to rapacious interest Glory leaves
Mankind, and every grace of life is gone.'

To this the power, whose vital radiance calls
From the brute mass of man an ordered world:
'Wait till the morning shines, and from the depth
Of Gothic darkness springs another day.

True, genius droops; the tender ancient taste
Of Beauty, then fresh blooming in her prime,
But faintly trembles through the callous soul;
And Grandeur, or of morals or of life,
Sinks into safe pursuits and creeping cares.
Even cautious virtue seems to stoop her flight,
And aged life to deem the generous deeds
Of youth romantic. Yet in cooler thought
Well reasoned, in researches piercing deep
Through nature's works, in profitable arts,
And all that calm experience can disclose,
(Slow guide, but sure) behold the world anew
Exalted rise, with other honours crowned;
And, where my Spirit wakes the finer power,
Athenian laurels still afresh shall bloom.

'Oblivious ages passed; while earth, forsook
By her best genii, lay to demons foul
And unchained furies an abandoned prey.
Contention led the van; first small of size,
But soon dilating to the skies she towers:
Then, wide as air, the livid fury spread,
And high her head above the stormy clouds
She blazed in omens, swelled the groaning winds
With wild surmises, battlings, sounds of war—
From land to land the maddening trumpet blew,
And poured her venom through the heart of man.
Shook to the pole, the north obeyed her call.
Forth rushed the bloody power of Gothic war,
War against human kind: Rapine, that led
Millions of raging robbers in his train:
Unlistening, barbarous force, to whom the sword
Is reason, honour, law: the foe of arts
By monsters followed, hideous to behold,
That claimed their place. Outrageous mixed with these
Another species of tyrannic rule;
Unknown before, whose cankerous shackles seized
The envenomed soul; a wilder Fury, she
Even o'er her Elder Sister tyrannized,
Or, if perchance agreed, inflamed her rage.
Dire was her train, and loud: the sable band,
Thundering—"Submit, ye Laity! ye profane!
Earth is the Lord's, and therefore ours; let kings
Allow the common claim, and half be theirs;
If not, behold! the sacred lightning flies!"
Scholastic Discord, with an hundred tongues,
For science uttering jangling words obscure,
Where frighted reason never yet could dwell.

Of peremptory feature, cleric pride,
Whose reddening cheek no contradiction bears;
And holy slander, his associate firm,
On whom the lying spirit still descends—
Mother of tortures! persecuting zeal,
High flashing in her hand the ready torch,
Or poniard bathed in unbelieving blood;
Hell's fiercest fiend! of saintly brow demure,
Assuming a celestial seraph's name,
While she beneath the blasphemous pretence
Of pleasing parent Heaven, the source of love!
Has wrought more horrors, more detested deeds
Than all the rest combined. Led on by her,
And wild of head to work her fell designs,
Came idiot Superstition; round with ears
Innumerous strowed, ten thousand monkish forms
With legends plied them, and with tenets, meant
To charm or scare the simple into slaves,
And poison reason; gross, she swallows all,
The most absurd believing ever most.
Broad o'er the whole her universal night,
The gloom still doubling, Ignorance diffused.

'Nought to be seen, but visionary monks
To councils strolling and embroiling creeds,
Banditti saints disturbing distant lands,
And unknown nations wandering for a home.
All lay reversed—the sacred arts of rule
Turned to flagitious leagues against mankind,
And arts of plunder more and more avowed;
Pure plain devotion to a solemn farce;
To holy dotage virtue, even to guile,
To murder, and a mockery of oaths;
Brave ancient freedom to the rage of slaves,
Proud of their state and fighting for their chains;
Dishonoured courage to the bravo's trade,
To civil broil; and glory to romance.
Thus human life, unhinged, to ruin reeled,
And giddy reason tottered on her throne.

'At last heaven's best inexplicable scheme,
Disclosing, bade new brightening eras smile.
The high command gone forth, Arts in my train,
And azure-mantled Science, swift we spread
A sounding pinion. Eager pity, mixed
With indignation, urged our downward flight.
On Latium first we stooped, for doubtful life
That panted, sunk beneath unnumbered woes.

Ah, poor Italia! what a bitter cup
Of vengeance hast thou drained! Goths, Vandals, Huns,
Lombards, barbarians broke from every land,
How many a ruffian form hast thou beheld!
What horrid jargons heard, where rage alone
Was all thy frighted ear could comprehend!
How frequent by the red inhuman hand,
Yet warm with brother's, husband's, father's blood,
Hast thou thy matrons and thy virgins seen
To violation dragged, and mingled death!
What conflagrations, earthquakes, ravage, floods,
Have turned thy cities into stony wilds;
And succourless and bare the poor remains
Of wretches forth to nature's common cast!
Added to these the still continual waste
Of inbred foes that on thy vitals prey,
And, double tyrants, seize the very soul.
Where hadst thou treasures for this rapine all?
These hungry myriads that thy bowels tore,
Heaped sack on sack, and buried in their rage
Wonders of art; whence this grey scene, a mine
Of more than gold becomes and orient gems,
Where Egypt, Greece, and Rome united glow.

'Here Sculpture, Painting, Architecture, bent
From ancient models to restore their arts,
Remained. A little trace we how they rose.

'Amid the hoary ruins, Sculpture first,
Deep digging, from the cavern dark and damp,
Their grave for ages, bade her marble race
Spring to new light. Joy sparkled in her eyes,
And old remembrance thrilled in every thought,
As she the pleasing resurrection saw.
In leaning site, respiring from his toils,
The well known hero who delivered Greece,
His ample chest all tempested with force,
Unconquerable reared. She saw the head,
Breathing the hero, small, of Grecian size,
Scarce more extensive than the sinewy neck;
The spreading shoulders, muscular and broad;
The whole a mass of swelling sinews, touched
Into harmonious shape; she saw, and joyed.
The yellow hunter, Meleager, raised
His beauteous front, and through the finished whole
Shows what ideas smiled of old in Greece.
Of raging aspect rushed impetuous forth
The Gladiator: pitiless his look,

And each keen sinew braced, the storm of war,
Ruffling, o'er all his nervous body frowns.
The dying other from the gloom she drew.
Supported on his shortened arm he leans,
Prone, agonizing; with incumbent fate
Heavy declines his head; yet dark beneath
The suffering feature sullen vengeance lours,
Shame, indignation, unaccomplished rage;
And still the cheated eye expects his fall.
All conquest-flushed from prostrate Python came
The quivered God. In graceful act he stands,
His arm extended with the slackened bow:
Light flows his easy robe, and fair displays
A manly-softened form. The bloom of gods
Seems youthful o'er the beardless cheek to wave:
His features yet heroic ardour warms;
And sweet subsiding to a native smile,
Mixed with the joy elating conquest gives,
A scattered frown exalts his matchless air.
On Flora moved; her full proportioned limbs
Rise through the mantle fluttering in the breeze.
The queen of love arose, as from the deep
She sprung in all the melting pomp of charms.
Bashful she bends, her well-taught look aside
Turns in enchanting guise, where dubious mix
Vain conscious beauty, a dissembled sense
Of modest shame, and slippery looks of love.
The gazer grows enamoured, and the stone,
As if exulting in its conquest, smiles.
So turned each limb, so swelled with softening art,
That the deluded eye the marble doubts.
At last her utmost masterpiece she found
That Maro fired—the miserable sire,
Wrapt with his sons in fate's severest grasp.
The serpents, twisting round, their stringent folds
Inextricable tie. Such passion here,
Such agonies, such bitterness of pain
Seem so to tremble through the tortured stone
That the touched heart engrosses all the view.
Almost unmarked the best proportions pass
That ever Greece beheld; and, seen alone,
On the rapt eye the imperious passions seize—
The father's double pangs, both for himself
And sons convulsed; to heaven his rueful look,
Imploring aid, and half accusing, cast;
His fell despair with indignation mixed,
As the strong curling monsters from his side
His full extended fury cannot tear.

More tender touched, with varied art, his sons
All the soft rage of younger passions show.
In a boy's helpless fate one sinks oppressed;
While, yet unpierced, the frighted other tries
His foot to steal out of the horrid twine.

'She bore no more, but straight from Gothic rust
Her chisel cleared, and dust and fragments drove
Impetuous round. Successive as it went
From son to son, with more enlivening touch,
From the brute rock it called the breathing form;
Till, in a legislator's awful grace
Dressed, Buonaroti bade a Moses rise,
And, looking love immense, a Saviour God.

'Of these observant, Painting felt the fire
Burn inward. Then ecstatic she diffused
The canvas, seized the pallet, with quick hand
The colours brewed; and on the void expanse
Her gay creation poured, her mimic world.
Poor was the manner of her eldest race,
Barren, and dry; just struggling from the taste
That had for ages scared in cloisters dim
The superstitious herd: yet glorious then
Were deemed their works; where undeveloped lay
The future wonders that enriched mankind,
And a new light and grace o'er Europe cast.
Arts gradual gather streams. Enlarging this,
To each his portion of her various gifts
The Goddess dealt, to none indulging all;
No, not to Raphael. At kind distance still
Perfection stands, like happiness, to tempt
The eternal chase. In elegant design,
Improving nature: in ideas, fair
Or great, extracted from the fine antique;
In attitude, expression, airs divine—
Her sons of Rome and Florence bore the prize.
To those of Venice she the magic art
Of colours melting into colours gave.
Theirs too it was by one embracing mass
Of light and shade, that settles round the whole,
Or varies tremulous from part to part,
O'er all a binding harmony to throw,
To raise the picture, and repose the sight.
The Lombard school, succeeding, mingled both.

'Meantime dread fanes and palaces around
Reared the magnific front. Music again

Her universal language of the heart
Renewed; and, rising from the plaintive vale,
To the full concert spread, and solemn quire.

'Even bigots smiled; to their protection took
Arts not their own, and from them borrowed pomp—
For in a tyrant's garden these awhile
May bloom, though freedom be their parent soil.

'And, now confessed, with gently-growing gleam
The morning shone, and westward streamed its light.
The muse awoke. Not sooner on the wing
Is the gay bird of dawn. Artless her voice,
Untaught and wild, yet warbled through the woods
Romantic lays. But as her northern course
She, with her tutor Science, in my train,
Ardent pursued, her strains more noble grew—
While reason drew the plan, the heart informed
The moral page, and fancy lent it grace.

'Rome and her circling deserts cast behind,
I passed not idle to my great sojourn.

'On Arno's fertile plain, where the rich vine
Luxuriant o'er Etrurian mountains roves,
Safe in the lap reposed of private bliss,
I small republics raised. Thrice happy they!
Had social freedom bound their peace, and arts,
Instead of ruling power, ne'er meant for them,
Employed their little cares, and saved their fate.

'Beyond the rugged Apennines, that roll
Far through Italian bounds their wavy tops,
My path too I with public blessings strowed:
Free states and cities, where the Lombard plain,
In spite of culture negligent and gross,
From her deep bosom pours unbidden joys,
And green o'er all the land a garden spreads.

'The barren rocks themselves beneath my foot
Relenting bloomed on the Ligurian shore.
Thick-swarming people there, like emmets, seized
Amid surrounding cliffs the scattered spots
Which nature left in her destroying rage,
Made their own fields, nor sighed for other lands.
There, in white prospect from the rocky hill
Gradual descending to the sheltered shore,
By me proud Genoa's marble turrets rose.

And, while my genuine spirit warmed her sons,
Beneath her Dorias, not unworthy, she
Vied for the trident of the narrow seas,
Ere Britain yet had opened all the main.

'Nor be the then triumphant state forgot,
Where, pushed from plundered earth, a remnant still,
Inspired by me, through the dark ages kept
Of my old Roman flame some sparks alive—
The seeming god-built city! which my hand
Deep in the bosom fixed of wondering seas.
Astonished mortals sailed with pleasing awe
Around the sea-girt walls, by Neptune fenced,
And down the briny street, where on each hand,
Amazing seen amid unstable waves,
The splendid palace shines, and rising tides,
The green steps marking, murmur at the door.
To this fair queen of Adria's stormy gulf,
The mart of nations! long obedient seas
Rolled all the treasure of the radiant East.
But now no more. Than one great tyrant worse
(Whose shared oppression lightens, as diffused),
Each subject tearing, many tyrants rose.
The least the proudest. Joined in dark cabal,
They, jealous, watchful, silent, and severe,
Cast o'er the whole indissoluble chains:
The softer shackles of luxurious ease
They likewise added, to secure their sway.
Thus Venice fainter shines; and Commerce thus,
Of toil impatient, flags the drooping sail.
Bursting, besides, his ancient bounds, he took
A larger circle; found another seat,
Opening a thousand ports, and charmed with toil
Whom nothing can dismay far other sons.

'The mountains then, clad with eternal snow,
Confessed my power. Deep as the rampart rocks
By nature thrown insuperable round,
I planted there a league of friendly states,
And bade plain freedom their ambition be.
There in the vale, where rural plenty fills
From lakes and meads and furrowed fields her horn,
Chief where the Leman pure emits the Rhone,
Rare to be seen! unguilty cities rise,
Cities of brothers formed—while equal life,
Accorded gracious with revolving power,
Maintains them free; and, in their happy streets,
Nor cruel deed nor misery is known.

For valour, faith, and innocence of life
Renowned, a rough laborious people there
Not only give the dreadful Alps to smile,
And press their culture on retiring snows;
But, to firm order trained and patient war,
They likewise know, beyond the nerve remiss
Of mercenary force, how to defend
The tasteful little their hard toil has earned,
And the proud arm of Bourbon to defy.

'Even, cheered by me, their shaggy mountains charm
More than or Gallic or Italian plains;
And sickening fancy oft, when absent long,
Pines to behold their Alpine views again—
The hollow-winding stream: the vale, fair-spread
Amid an amphitheatre of hills,
Whence, vapour-winged, the sudden tempest springs;
From steep to steep ascending, the gay train
Of fogs thick-rolled into romantic shapes;
The flitting cloud, against the summit dashed;
And, by the sun illumined, pouring bright
A gemmy shower—hung o'er amazing rocks,
The mountain ash, and solemn sounding pine;
The snow-fed torrent, in white mazes tossed
Down to the clear ethereal lake below;
And, high o'ertopping all the broken scene,
The mountain fading into sky, where shines
On winter winter shivering; and whose top
Licks from their cloudy magazine the snows.

'From these descending, as I waved my course
O'er vast Germania, the ferocious nurse
Of hardy men, and hearts affronting death,
I gave some favoured cities there to lift
A nobler brow, and through their swarming streets,
More busy, wealthy, cheerful, and alive,
In each contented face to look my soul.

'Thence the loud Baltic passing, black with storm,
To wintry Scandinavia's utmost bound—
There I the manly race, the parent hive
Of the mixed kingdoms, formed into a state
More regularly free. By keener air
Their genius purged, and tempered hard by frost,
Tempest and toil their nerves, the sons of those
Whose only terror was a bloodless death,
They, wise and dauntless, still sustain my cause.
Yet there I fixed not. Turning to the south,

The whispering zephyrs sighed at my delay.'

Here, with the shifted vision, burst my joy:
'O the dear prospect! O majestic view!
See Britain's empire! lo! the watery vast
Wide-waves, diffusing the cerulean plain.
And now, methinks, like clouds at distance seen,
Emerging white from deeps of ether, dawn
My kindred cliffs; whence, wafted in the gale,
Ineffable, a secret sweetness breathes.
Goddess, forgive!—My heart, surprised, o'erflows
With filial fondness for the land you bless.'

As parents to a child complacent deign
Approvance, the celestial Brightness smiled;
Then thus—'As o'er the wave-resounding deep
To my near reign, the happy isle, I steered
With easy wing—behold! from surge to surge
Stalked the tremendous Genius of the Deep.
Around him clouds in mingled tempest hung;
Thick flashing meteors crowned his starry head;
And ready thunder reddened in his hand,
Or from it streamed compressed the gloomy cloud.
Where'er he looked, the trembling waves recoiled.
He needs but strike the conscious flood, and shook
From shore to shore, in agitation dire,
It works his dreadful will. To me his voice
(Like that hoarse blast that round the cavern howls,
Mixed with the murmurs of the falling main),
Addressed, began—"By fate commissioned, go,
My sister-goddess now, to yon blest isle,
Henceforth the partner of my rough domain.
All my dread walks to Britons open lie.
Those that refulgent, or with rosy morn
Or yellow evening, flame; those that, profuse
Drunk by equator suns, severely shine;
Or those that, to the poles approaching, rise
In billows rolling into Alps of ice.
Even, yet untouched by daring keel, be theirs
The vast Pacific—that on other worlds,
Their future conquest, rolls resounding tides.
Long I maintained inviolate my reign;
Nor Alexanders me, nor Caesars braved.
Still in the crook of shore the coward sail
Till now low crept; and peddling commerce plied
Between near joining lands. For Britons, chief,
It was reserved, with star-directed prow,
To dare the middle deep, and drive assured

To distant nations through the pathless main.
Chief, for their fearless hearts the glory waits,
Long months from land, while the black stormy night
Around them rages, on the groaning mast
With unshook knee to know their giddy way;
To sing, unquelled, amid the lashing wave;
To laugh at danger. Theirs the triumph be,
By deep invention's keen pervading eye,
The heart of courage, and the hand of toil,
Each conquered ocean staining with their blood,
Instead of treasure robbed by ruffian war,
Round social earth to circle fair exchange
And bind the nations in a golden chain.
To these I honoured stoop. Rushing to light
A race of men behold! whose daring deeds
Will in renown exalt my nameless plains
O'er those of fabling earth, as hers to mine
In terror yield. Nay, could my savage heart
Such glories check, their unsubmitting soul
Would all my fury brave, my tempest climb,
And might in spite of me my kingdom force."
Here, waiting no reply, the shadowy Power
Eased the dark sky, and to the deeps returned—
While the loud thunder rattling from his hand,
Auspicious, shook opponent Gallia's shore.

'Of this encounter glad, my way to land
I quick pursued, that from the smiling sea
Received me joyous. Loud acclaims were heard;
And music, more than mortal, warbling, filled
With pleased astonishment the labouring hind,
Who for a while the unfinished furrow left,
And let the listening steer forget his toil.
Unseen by grosser eye, Britannia breathed,
And her aerial train, these sounds of joy.
For of old time, since first the rushing flood,
Urged by almighty power, this favoured isle
Turned flashing from the continent aside,
Indented shore to shore responsive still,
Its guardian she—the Goddess, whose staid eye
Beams the dark azure of the doubtful dawn.
Her tresses, like a flood of softened light
Through clouds imbrowned, in waving circles play.
Warm on her cheek sits beauty's brightest rose.
Of high demeanour, stately, shedding grace
With every motion. Full her rising chest;
And new ideas from her finished shape
Charmed Sculpture taking might improve her art.

Such the fair guardian of an isle that boasts,
Profuse as vernal blooms, the fairest dames.
High shining on the promontory's brow,
Awaiting me, she stood with hope inflamed,
By my mixed spirit burning in her sons,
To firm, to polish, and exalt the state.

'The native genii round her radiant smiled.
Courage, of soft deportment, aspect calm,
Unboastful, suffering long, and, till provoked,
As mild and harmless as the sporting child;
But, on just reason, once his fury roused,
No lion springs more eager to his prey—
Blood is a pastime; and his heart, elate,
Knows no depressing fear. That Virtue known
By the relenting look, whose equal heart
For others feels as for another self—
Of various name, as various objects wake,
Warm into action, the kind sense within:
Whether the blameless poor, the nobly maimed,
The lost to reason, the declined in life,
The helpless young that kiss no mother's hand,
And the grey second infancy of age
She gives in public families to live,
A sight to gladden heaven! whether she stands
Fair-beckoning at the hospitable gate,
And bids the stranger take repose and joy;
Whether, to solace honest labour, she
Rejoices those that make the land rejoice;
Or whether to philosophy and arts
(At once the basis and the finished pride
Of government and life) she spreads her hand,
Nor knows her gift profuse, nor seems to know,
Doubling her bounty, that she gives at all.
Justice to these her awful presence joined,
The mother of the state! No low revenge,
No turbid passions in her breast ferment:
Tender, serene, compassionate of vice,
As the last woe that can afflict mankind,
She punishment awards; yet of the good
More piteous still, and of the suffering whole,
Awards it firm. So fair her just decree,
That, in his judging peers, each on himself
Pronounces his own doom. O happy land!
Where reigns alone this justice of the free!
Mid the bright group, Sincerity his front,
Diffusive, reared; his pure untroubled eye
The fount of truth. The Thoughtful Power, apart,

Now pensive cast on earth his fixed regard,
Now, touched celestial, launched it on the sky.
The genius he whence Britain shines supreme,
The land of light and rectitude of mind.
He, too, the fire of fancy feeds intense,
With all the train of passions thence derived—
Not kindling quick, a noisy transient blaze,
But gradual, silent, lasting, and profound.
Near him Retirement, pointing to the shade,
And Independence stood—the generous pair
That simple life, the quiet-whispering grove,
And the still raptures of the free-born soul
To cates prefer by virtue bought, not earned,
Proudly prefer them to the servile pomp
And to the heart-embittered joys of slaves.
Or should the latter, to the public scene
Demanded, quit his silvan friend awhile—
Nought can his firmness shake, nothing seduce
His zeal, still active for the commonweal;
Nor stormy tyrants, nor corruption's tools,
Foul ministers, dark-working by the force
Of secret-sapping gold. All their vile arts,
Their shameful honours, their perfidious gifts,
He greatly scorns; and, if he must betray
His plundered country or his power resign,
A moment's parley were eternal shame;
Illustrious into private life again,
From dirty levees he unstained ascends,
And firm in senates stands the patriot's ground,
Or draws new vigour in the peaceful shade.
Aloof the Bashful Virtue hovered coy,
Proving by sweet distrust distrusted worth.
Rough Labour closed the train: and in his hand
Rude, callous, sinew-swelled, and black with toil,
Came manly Indignation. Sour he seems,
And more than seems, by lawless pride assailed;
Yet kind at heart, and just, and generous; there
No vengeance lurks, no pale insidious gall;
Even in the very luxury of rage,
He softening can forgive a gallant foe;
The nerve, support, and glory of the land!
Nor be Religion, rational and free,
Here passed in silence; whose enraptured eye
Sees heaven with earth connected, human things
Linked to divine: who not from servile fear,
By rites for some weak tyrant incense fit,
The God of love adores, but from a heart
Effusing gladness, into pleasing awe

That now astonished swells, now in a calm
Of fearless confidence that smiles serene;
That lives devotion, one continual hymn,
And then most grateful when heaven's bounty most
Is right enjoyed. This ever cheerful power
O'er the raised circle rayed superior day.

'I joyed to join the virtues, whence my reign
O'er Albion was to rise. Each cheering each,
And, like the circling planets from the sun,
All borrowing beams from me, a heightened zeal
Impatient fired us to commence our toils,
Or pleasures rather. Long the pungent time
Passed not in mutual hails; but, through the land
Darting our light, we shone the fogs away.

'The virtues conquer with a single look.
Such grace, such beauty, such victorious light,
Live in their presence, stream in every glance,
That the soul won, enamoured, and refined,
Grows their own image, pure ethereal flame.
Hence the foul demons that oppose our reign
Would still from us deluded mortals wrap;
Or in gross shades they drown the visual ray,
Or by the fogs of prejudice, where mix
Falsehood and truth confounded, foil the sense
With vain refracted images of bliss.
But chief around the court of flattered kings
They roll the dusky rampart, wall o'er wall
Of darkness pile, and with their thickest shade
Secure the throne. No savage Alp, the den
Of wolves and bears and monstrous things obscene,
That vex the swain and waste the country round,
Protected lies beneath a deeper cloud:
Yet there we sometimes send a searching ray.
As, at the sacred opening of the morn,
The prowling race retire; so, pierced severe,
Before our potent blaze these demons fly,
And all their works dissolve—the whispered tale,
That, like the fabling Nile, no fountain knows;
Fair-faced deceit, whose wily conscious eye
Ne'er looks direct; the tongue that licks the dust,
But, when it safely dares, as prompt to sting;
Smooth crocodile destruction, whose fell tears
Ensnare; the Janus—face of courtly pride—
One to superiors heaves submissive eyes,
On hapless worth the other scowls disdain;
Cheeks that for some weak tenderness, alone,

Some virtuous slip, can wear a blush; the laugh
Profane, when midnight bowls disclose the heart,
At starving virtue and at virtue's fools;
Determined to be broke, the plighted faith;
Nay more, the godless oath, that knows no ties:
Soft-buzzing slander-silky moths, that eat
An honest name: the harpy hand and maw
Of avaricious luxury, who makes
The throne his shelter, venal laws his fort,
And, by his service, who betrays his king.

'Now turn your view, and mark from Celtic night
To present grandeur how my Britain rose.

'Bold were those Britons, who, the careless sons
Of nature, roamed the forest-bounds, at once
Their verdant city, high-embowering fane,
And the gay circle of their woodland wars:
For by the Druid taught, that death but shifts
The vital scene, they that prime fear despised;
And, prone to rush on steel, disdained to spare
An ill-saved life that must again return.
Erect from nature's hand, by tyrant force
And still more tyrant custom unsubdued,
Man knows no master save creating heaven,
Or such as choice and common good ordain.
This general sense, with which the nations I
Promiscuous fire, in Britons burned intense,
Of future times prophetic. Witness, Rome,
Who saw'st thy Caesar from the naked land,
Whose only fort was British hearts, repelled,
To seek Pharsalian wreaths. Witness the toil,
The blood of ages, bootless to secure
Beneath an empire's yoke a stubborn isle,
Disputed hard and never quite subdued.
The north remained untouched, where those who scorned
To stoop retired; and, to their keen effort
Yielding at last, recoiled the Roman power.
In vain, unable to sustain the shock,
From sea to sea desponding legions raised
The wall immense—and yet, on summer's eve,
While sport his lambkins round, the shepherd's gaze.
Continual o'er it burst the northern storm;
As often, checked, receded—threatening hoarse
A swift return. But the devouring flood
No more endured control, when, to support
The last remains of empire, was recalled
The weary Roman, and the Briton lay

Unnerved, exhausted, spiritless, and sunk.
Great proof! how men enfeeble into slaves.
The sword behind him flashed; before him roared,
Deaf to his woes, the deep. Forlorn, around
He rolled his eye—not sparkling ardent flame
As when Caractacus to battle led
Silurian swains, and Boadicea taught
Her raging troops the miseries of slaves.

'Then (sad relief!) from the bleak coast that hears
The German Ocean roar, deep-blooming, strong,
And yellow-haired, the blue-eyed Saxon came.
He came implored, but came with other aim
Than to protect. For conquest and defence
Suffices the same arm. With the fierce race
Poured in a fresh invigorating stream,
Blood, where unquelled a mighty spirit glowed.
Rash war and perilous battle their delight;
And immature, and red with glorious wounds,
Unpeaceful death their choice-deriving thence
A right to feast and drain immortal bowls
In Odin's hall, whose blazing roof resounds
The genial uproar of those shades who fall
In desperate fight or by some brave attempt;
And, though more polished times the martial creed
Disown, yet still the fearless habit lives.
Nor were the surly gifts of war their all.
Wisdom was likewise theirs, indulgent laws,
The calm gradations of art-nursing peace,
And matchless orders, the deep basis still
On which ascends my British reign. Untamed
To the refining subtleties of slaves,
They brought a happy government along;
Formed by that freedom which, with secret voice,
Impartial nature teaches all her sons,
And which of old through the whole Scythian mass
I strong inspired. Monarchical their state,
But prudently confined, and mingled wise
Of each harmonious power: only, too much,
Imperious war into their rule infused,
Prevailed their general-king and chieftain-thanes.

'In many a field, by civil fury stained,
Bled the discordant Heptarchy; and long
(Educing good from ill) the battle groaned
Ere, blood-cemented, Anglo-Saxons saw
Egbert and peace on one united throne.

'No sooner dawned the fair disclosing calm
Of brighter days, when lo! the north anew,
With stormy nations black, on England poured
Woes the severest e'er a people felt.
The Danish raven, lured by annual prey,
Hung o'er the land incessant. Fleet on fleet
Of barbarous pirates, unremitting tore
The miserable coast. Before them stalked,
Far seen, the demon of devouring flame;
Rapine, and murder, all with blood besmeared,
Without or ear or eye or feeling heart:
While close behind them marched the sallow power
Of desolating famine, who delights
In grass-grown cities and in desert fields;
And purple-spotted pestilence, by whom
Even friendship scared, in sickening horror sinks
Each social sense and tenderness of life.
Fixing at last, the sanguinary race
Spread, from the Humber's loud resounding shore
To where the Thames devolves his gentle maze,
And with superior arm the Saxon awed.
But superstition first, and monkish dreams
And monk-directed cloister-seeking kings
Had eat away his vigour, eat away
His edge of courage, and depressed the soul
Of conquering freedom which he once respired.
Thus cruel ages passed; and rare appeared
White-mantled Peace, exulting o'er the vale;
As when, with Alfred, from the wilds she came
To policed cities and protected plains.
Thus by degrees the Saxon empire sunk,
Then set entire in Hastings' bloody field.

'Compendious war! (on Britain's glory bent,
So fate ordained) in that decisive day,
The haughty Norman seized at once an isle
For which through many a century in vain
The Roman, Saxon, Dane had toiled and bled.
Of Gothic nations this the final burst;
And, mixed the genius of these people all,
Their virtues mixed in one exalted stream,
Here the rich tide of English blood grew full.

'Awhile my spirit slept; the land awhile,
Affrighted, drooped beneath despotic rage.
Instead of Edward's equal gentle laws,
The furious victor's partial will prevailed.
All prostrate lay; and, in the secret shade,

Deep-stung but fearful, Indignation gnashed
His teeth. Of freedom, property, despoiled,
And of their bulwark, arms; with castles crushed,
With ruffians quartered o'er the bridled land—
The shivering wretches, at the curfew sound,
Dejected shrunk into their sordid beds,
And, through the mournful gloom, of ancient times
Mused sad, or dreamt of better. Even to feed
A tyrant's idle sport the peasant starved:
To the wild herd the pasture of the tame,
The cheerful hamlet, spiry town was given,
And the brown forest roughened wide around.

'But this so dead, so vile submission long
Endured not. Gathering force, my gradual flame
Shook off the mountain of tyrannic sway.
Unused to bend, impatient of control,
Tyrants themselves the common tyrant checked.
The church, by kings intractable and fierce,
Denied her portion of the plundered state,
Or, tempted by the timorous and weak,
To gain new ground first taught their rapine law.
The Barons next a nobler league began,
Both those of English and of Norman race,
In one fraternal nation blended now,
The nation of the free! Pressed by a band
Of Patriots, ardent as the summer's noon
That looks delighted on, the tyrant see!
Mark! how with feigned alacrity he bears
His strong reluctance down, his dark revenge,
And gives the charter by which life indeed
Becomes of price, a glory to be man.

'Through this, and through succeeding reigns affirmed
These long-contested rights, the wholesome winds
Of opposition hence began to blow;
And often since have lent the country life.
Before their breath corruption's insect-blights,
The darkening clouds of evil counsel, fly;
Or, should they sounding swell, a putrid court,
A pestilential ministry, they purge,
And ventilated states renew their bloom.

'Though with the tempered monarchy here mixed
Aristocratic sway, the people still,
Flattered by this or that, as interest leaned,
No full protection knew. For me reserved,
And for my commons, was that glorious turn.

They crowned my first attempt—in senates rose,
The fort of freedom! Slow till then, alone
Had worked that general liberty, that soul
Which generous nature breathes, and which, when left
By me to bondage was corrupted Rome,
I through the northern nations wide diffused.
Hence many a people, fierce with freedom, rushed
From the rude iron regions of the north,
To Libyan deserts swarm protruding swarm,
And poured new spirit through a slavish world.
Yet, o'er these Gothic states, the king and chiefs
Retained the high prerogative of war,
And with enormous property engrossed
The mingled power. But on Britannia's shore
Now present, I to raise my reign began
By raising the democracy, the third
And broadest bulwark of the guarded state.
Then was the full the perfect plan disclosed
Of Britain's matchless constitution, mixed
Of mutual checking and supporting powers,
King, lords, and commons; nor the name of free
Deserving, while the vassal—many drooped:
For, since the moment of the whole they form,
So, as depressed or raised, the balance they
Of public welfare and of glory cast.
Mark from this period the continual proof.

'When kings of narrow genius, minion-rid,
Neglecting faithful worth for fawning slaves;
Proudly regardless of their people's plaints,
And poorly passive of insulting foes;
Double, not prudent, obstinate, not firm,
Their mercy fear, necessity their faith;
Instead of generous fire, presumptuous, hot,
Rash to resolve, and slothful to perform;
Tyrants at once and slaves, imperious, mean,
To want rapacious joining shameful waste;
By counsels weak and wicked, easy roused
To paltry schemes of absolute command,
To seek their splendour in their sure disgrace,
And in a broken ruined people wealth—
When such o'ercast the state, no bond of love,
No heart, no soul, no unity, no nerve
Combined the loose disjointed public, lost
To fame abroad, to happiness at home.

'But when an Edward, and a Henry breathed
Through the charmed whole one all-exerting soul;

Drawn sympathetic from his dark retreat,
When wide-attracted merit round them glowed;
When counsels just, extensive, generous, firm,
Amid the maze of state, determined kept
Some ruling point in view; when, on the stock
Of public good and glory grafted, spread
Their palms, their laurels—or, if thence they strayed,
Swift to return, and patient of restraint;
When regal state, pre-eminence of place,
They scorned to deem pre-eminence of ease,
To be luxurious drones, that only rob
The busy hive; as in distinction, power,
Indulgence, honour, and advantage first—
When they too claimed in virtue, danger, toil
Superior rank, with equal hand prepared
To guard the subject and to quell the foe:
When such with me their vital influence shed,
No muttered grievance, hopeless sigh was heard;
No foul distrust through wary senates ran,
Confined their bounty, and their ardour quenched;
On aid, unquestioned, liberal aid was given;
Safe in their conduct, by their valour fired,
Fond where they led victorious armies rushed;
And Cressy, Poitiers, Agincourt proclaim
What kings supported by almighty love
And people fired with liberty can do.

'Be veiled the savage reigns, when kindred rage
The numerous once Plantagenets devoured,
A race to vengeance vowed! and when, oppressed
By private feuds, almost extinguished lay
My quivering flame. But, in the next, behold!
A cautious tyrant lend it oil anew.

'Proud, dark, suspicious, brooding o'er his gold,
As how to fix his throne he jealous cast
His crafty views around; pierced with a ray,
Which on his timid mind I darted full,
He marked the barons of excessive sway,
At pleasure making and unmaking kings;
And hence, to crush these petty tyrants, planned
A law, that let them, by the silent waste
Of luxury, their landed wealth diffuse,
And with that wealth their implicated power.
By soft degrees a mighty change ensued,
Even working to this day. With streams, deduced
From these diminished floods, the country smiled.
As, when impetuous from the snow-heaped Alps,

To vernal suns relenting, pours the Rhine,
While undivided, oft with wasteful sweep
He foams along; but through Batavian meads,
Branched into fair canals, indulgent flows,
Waters a thousand fields, and culture, trade,
Towns, meadows, gliding ships, and villas mixed,
A rich, a wondrous landscape rises round.

'His furious son the soul-enslaving chain,
Which many a doting venerable age
Had link by link strong twisted round the land,
Shook off. No longer could be borne a power,
From heaven pretended, to deceive, to void
Each solemn tie, to plunder without bounds,
To curb the generous soul, to fool mankind;
And, wild at last, to plunge into a sea
Of blood and horror. The returning light,
That first through Wickliff streaked the priestly gloom,
Now burst in open day. Bared to the blaze,
Forth from the haunts of superstition crawled
Her motley sons, fantastic figures all;
And, wide dispersed, their useless fetid wealth
In graceful labour bloomed, and fruits of peace.

'Trade, joined to these, on every sea displayed
A daring canvas, poured with every tide
A golden flood. From other worlds were rolled
The guilty glittering stores, whose fatal charms,
By the plain Indian happily despised,
Yet worked his woe; and to the blissful groves,
Where nature lived herself among her sons,
And innocence and joy for ever dwelt,
Drew rage unknown to pagan climes before,
The worst the zeal-inflamed barbarian drew.
Be no such horrid commerce, Britain, thine! 920
But want for want with mutual aid supply.

'The commons thus enriched, and powerful grown,
Against the barons weighed. Eliza then,
Amid these doubtful motions steady, gave
The beam to fix. She, like the secret eye
That never closes on a guarded world,
So sought, so marked, so seized the public good
That, self-supported, without one ally,
She awed her inward, quelled her circling foes.
Inspired by me, beneath her sheltering arm,
In spite of raging universal sway
And raging seas repressed, the Belgic states,

My bulwark on the continent, arose.
Matchless in all the spirit of her days!
With confidence unbounded, fearless love
Elate, her fervent people waited gay,
Cheerful demanded the long threatened fleet,
And dashed the pride of Spain around their isle.
Nor ceased the British thunder here to rage:
The deep, reclaimed, obeyed its awful call;
In fire and smoke Iberian ports involved,
The trembling foe even to the centre shook
Of their new conquered world, and, skulking, stole
By veering winds their Indian treasure home.
Meantime, peace, plenty, justice, science, arts,
With softer laurels crowned her happy reign.

'As yet uncircumscribed the regal power,
And wild and vague prerogative remained—
A wide voracious gulf, where swallowed oft
The helpless subject lay. This to reduce
To the just limit was my great effort.

'By means that evil seem to narrow man
Superior beings work their mystic will:
From storm and trouble thus a settled calm,
At last, effulgent, o'er Britannia smiled.
'The gathering tempest, heaven-commissioned, came,
Came in the prince, who, drunk with flattery, dreamt
His vain pacific counsels ruled the world;
Though scorned abroad, bewildered in a maze
Of fruitless treaties; while at home enslaved,
And by a worthless crew insatiate drained,
He lost his people's confidence and love:
Irreparable loss! whence crowns become
An anxious burden. Years inglorious passed:
Triumphant Spain the vengeful draught enjoyed—
Abandoned Frederick pined, and Raleigh bled.
But nothing that to these internal broils,
That rancour, he began; while lawless sway
He, with his slavish doctors, tried to rear
On metaphysic, on enchanted ground,
And all the mazy quibbles of the schools:
As if for one, and sometimes for the worst,
Heaven had mankind in vengeance only made.
Vain the pretence! not so the dire effect,
The fierce, the foolish discord thence derived,
That tears the country still, by party rage
And ministerial clamour kept alive.
In action weak, and for the wordy war

Best fitted, faint this prince pursued his claim—
Content to teach the subject herd, how great,
How sacred he! how despicable they!

'But his unyielding son these doctrines drank
With all a bigot's rage (who never damps
By reasoning his fire); and what they taught,
Warm and tenacious, into practice pushed.
Senates, in vain, their kind restraint applied:
The more they struggled to support the laws,
His justice-dreading ministers the more
Drove him beyond their bounds. Tired with the check
Of faithful love, and with the flattery pleased
Of false designing guilt, the fountain he
Of public wisdom and of justice shut.
Wide mourned the land. Straight to the voted aid
Free, cordial, large, of never-failing source,
The illegal imposition followed harsh,
With execration given, or ruthless squeezed
From an insulted people by a band
Of the worst ruffians, those of tyrant power.
Oppression walked at large, and poured abroad
Her unrelenting train—informers, spies,
Bloodhounds, that sturdy freedom to the grave
Pursue; projectors of aggrieving schemes,
Commerce to load for unprotected seas,
To sell the starving many to the few,
And drain a thousand ways the exhausted land.
Even from that place whence healing peace should flow,
And gospel truth, inhuman bigots shed
Their poison round; and on the venal bench,
Instead of justice, party held the scale,
And violence the sword. Afflicted years,
Too patient, felt at last their vengeance full.

'Mid the low murmurs of submissive fear
And mingled rage my Hampden raised his voice,
And to the laws appealed; the laws no more
In judgement sat, behoved some other ear.
When instant from the keen resentive north,
By long oppression by religion roused,
The guardian army came. Beneath its wing
Was called, though meant to furnish hostile aid,
The more than Roman senate. There a flame
Broke out that cleared, consumed, renewed the land.
In deep emotion hurled, nor Greece nor Rome
Indignant bursting from a tyrant's chain,
While, full of me, each agitated soul

Strung every nerve and flamed—in every eye,
Had e'er beheld such light and heat combined!
Such heads and hearts! such dreadful zeal, led on
By calm majestic wisdom, taught its course
What nuisance to devour; such wisdom fired
With unabating zeal, and aimed sincere
To clear the weedy state, restore the laws,
And for the future to secure their sway.

'This then the purpose of my mildest sons.
But man is blind. A nation once inflamed
(Chief, should the breath of factious fury blow,
With the wild rage of mad enthusiast swelled)
Not easy cools again. From breast to breast,
From eye to eye, the kindling passions mix
In heightened blaze; and, ever wise and just,
High heaven to gracious ends directs the storm.
Thus in one conflagration Britain wrapt,
And by confusion's lawless sons despoiled,
King, lords, and commons, thundering to the ground,
Successive, rushed—Lo! from their ashes rose,
Gay-beaming radiant youth, the phoenix State.

'The grievous yoke of vassalage, the yoke
Of private life, lay by those flames dissolved;
And, from the wasteful, the luxurious king,
Was purchased that which taught the young to bend.
Stronger restored, the commons taxed the whole,
And built on that eternal rock their power.
The crown, of its hereditary wealth
Despoiled, on senates more dependent grew,
And they more frequent, more assured. Yet lived,
And in full vigour spread, that bitter root,
The passive doctrines—by their patrons first
Opposed ferocious, when they touch themselves.

'This wild delusive cant; the rash cabal
Of hungry courtiers, ravenous for prey
The bigot, restless in a double chain
To bind anew the land; the constant need
Of finding faithless means, of shifting forms,
And flattering senates to supply his waste;
These tore some moments from the careless prince,
And in his breast awaked the kindred plan.
By dangerous softness long he mined his way—
By subtle arts, dissimulation deep,
By sharing what corruption showered profuse,
By breathing wide the gay licentious plague,

And pleasing manners, fitted to deceive.

'At last subsided the delirious joy,
On whose high billow, from the saintly reign,
The nation drove too far. A pensioned king,
Against his country bribed by Gallic gold;
The port pernicious sold, the Scylla since
And fell Charybdis of the British seas;
Freedom attacked abroad, with surer blow
To cut it off at home; the saviour-league
Of Europe broke; the progress even advanced
Of universal sway, which to reduce
Such seas of blood and treasure Britain cost;
The millions, by a generous people given,
Or squandered vile, or to corrupt, disgrace,
And awe the land with forces not their own
Employed; the darling church herself betrayed—
All these, broad glaring, oped the general eye,
And waked my spirit, the resisting soul.

'Mild was, at first, and half ashamed, the check
Of senates, shook from the fantastic dream
Of absolute submission, tenets vile!
Which slaves would blush to own, and which, reduced
To practise, always honest nature shock.
Not even the mask removed, and the fierce front
Of tyranny disclosed; nor trampled laws;
Nor seized each badge of freedom through the land;
Nor Sidney bleeding for the unpublished page;
Nor on the bench avowed corruption placed,
And murderous rage itself, in Jefferies' form;
Nor endless acts of arbitrary power,
Cruel, and false, could raise the public arm.
Distrustful, scattered, of combining chiefs
Devoid, and dreading blind rapacious war,
The patient public turns not till impelled
To the near verge of ruin. Hence I roused
The bigot king, and hurried fated on
His measures immature. But chief his zeal,
Out-flaming Rome herself, portentous scared
The troubled nation: Mary's horrid days
To fancy bleeding rose, and the dire glare
Of Smithfield lightened in its eyes anew.
Yet silence reigned. Each on another scowled
Rueful amazement, pressing down his rage—
As, mustering vengeance, the deep thunder frowns,
Awfully still, waiting the high command
To spring. Straight from his country, Europe, saved

To save Britannia, lo! my darling son,
Than hero more! the patriot of mankind!
Immortal Nassau came. I hushed the deep
By demons roused, and bade the listed winds,
Still shifting as behoved, with various breath
Waft the deliverer to the longing shore.
See, wide alive, the foaming channel bright
With swelling sails and all the pride of war!
Delightful view when justice draws the sword!
And mark, diffusing ardent soul around
And sweet contempt of death, my streaming flag!
Even adverse navies blessed the binding gale,
Kept down the glad acclaim, and silent joyed.
Arrived, the pomp and not the waste of arms
His progress marked. The faint opposing host
For once, in yielding their best victory found,
And by desertion proved exalted faith:
While his the bloodless conquest of the heart,
Shouts without groan, and triumph without war.

'Then dawned the period destined to confine
The surge of wild prerogative, to raise
A mound restraining its imperious rage,
And bid the raving deep no farther flow.
Nor were, without that fence, the swallowed state
Better than Belgian plains without their dykes,
Sustaining weighty seas. This, often saved
By more than human hand, the public saw,
And seized the white-winged moment. Pleased to yield
Destructive power, a wise heroic prince
Even lent his aid. Thrice happy! did they know
Their happiness, Britannia's bounded kings.
What though not theirs the boast in dungeon glooms
To plunge bold freedom; or to cheerless wilds
To drive him from the cordial face of friend;
Or fierce to strike him at the midnight hour
By mandate blind—not justice, that delights
To dare the keenest eye of open day?
What though no glory to control the laws
And make injurious will their only rule
They deem it? What though, tools of wanton power,
Pestiferous armies swarm not at their call?
What though they give not a relentless crew
Of civil furies, proud oppression's fangs!
To tear at pleasure the dejected land,
With starving labour pampering idle waste?
To clothe the naked, feed the hungry, wipe
The guiltless tear from lone affliction's eye,

To raise hid merit, set the alluring light
Of virtue high to view, to nourish arts,
Direct the thunder of an injured state,
Make a whole glorious people sing for joy,
Bless humankind, and through the downward depth
Of future times to spread that better sun
Which lights up British soul—for deeds like these,
The dazzling fair career unbounded lies;
While (still superior bliss!) the dark abrupt
Is kindly barred, the precipice of ill
O luxury divine! O poor to this,
Ye giddy glories of despotic thrones!
By this, by this indeed, is imaged heaven,
By boundless good without the power of ill.

'And now behold! exalted as the cope
That swells immense o'er many-peopled earth,
And like it free, my fabric stands complete,
The palace of the laws. To the four heavens
Four gates impartial thrown, unceasing crowds,
With kings themselves the hearty peasant mixed,
Pour urgent in. And though to different ranks
Responsive place belongs, yet equal spreads
The sheltering roof o'er all; while plenty flows,
And glad contentment echoes round the whole.
Ye floods, descend! Ye winds, confirming, blow!
Nor outward tempest, nor corrosive time,
Nought but the felon undermining hand
Of dark corruption, can its frame dissolve,
And lay the toil of ages in the dust.'

THE CONTENTS OF PART V

The author addresses the Goddess of Liberty, marking the happiness and grandeur of Great Britain, as arising from her influence, to verse 87. She resumes her discourse, and points out the chief Virtues which are necessary to maintain her establishment there, to verse 373. Recommends, as its last ornament and finishing, Sciences, Fine Arts, and Public works; the encouragement of these urged from the example of France, though under a despotic government, to verse 548. The whole concludes with a prospect of future times, given by the Goddess of Liberty: this described by the author as it passes in vision before him.

PART V. THE PROSPECT

[Published, 1736]

Here interposing, as the Goddess paused;—
'O blest Britannia! in thy presence blest,
Thou guardian of mankind! whence spring alone
All human grandeur, happiness, and fame;
For toil, by thee protected, feels no pain,
The poor man's lot with milk and honey flows,
And, gilded with thy rays, even death looks gay.
Let other lands the potent blessings boast
Of more exalting suns. Let Asia's woods,
Untended, yield the vegetable fleece:
And let the little insect-artist form,
On higher life intent, its silken tomb.
Let wondering rocks, in radiant birth, disclose
The various tinctured children of the sun.
From the prone beam let more delicious fruits
A flavour drink that in one piercing taste
Bids each combine. Let Gallic vineyards burst
With floods of joy; with mild balsamic juice
The Tuscan olive. Let Arabia breathe
Her spicy gales, her vital gums distil.
Turbid with gold, let southern rivers flow,
And orient floods draw soft, o'er pearls, their maze.
Let Afric vaunt her treasures; let Peru
Deep in her bowels her own ruin breed,
The yellow traitor that her bliss betrayed—
Unequalled bliss I—and to unequalled rage!
Yet nor the gorgeous east, nor golden south,
Nor, in full prime, that new discovered world
Where flames the falling day, in wealth and praise
Shall with Britannia vie while, Goddess, she
Derives her praise from thee, her matchless charms.
Her hearty fruits the hand of freedom own;
And warm with culture, her thick clustering fields,
Prolific teem. Eternal verdure crowns
Her meads; her gardens smile eternal spring.
She gives the hunter-horse, unquelled by toil,
Ardent to rush into the rapid chase;
She, whitening o'er her downs, diffusive pours
Unnumbered flocks; she weaves the fleecy robe,
That wraps the nations; she to lusty droves
The richest pasture spreads; and, hers, deep-wave
Autumnal seas of pleasing plenty round.
These her delights—and by no baneful herb,
No darting tiger, no grim lion's glare,
No fierce-descending wolf, no serpent rolled
In spires immense progressive o'er the land
Disturbed. Enlivening these, add cities full

Of wealth, of trade, of cheerful toiling crowds;
Add thriving towns; add villages and farms,
Innumerous sowed along the lively vale,
Where bold unrivalled peasants happy dwell;
Add ancient seats, with venerable oaks
Embosomed high, while kindred floods below
Wind through the mead; and those of modern hand
More pompous add, that splendid shine afar.
Need I her limpid lakes, her rivers name,
Where swarm the finny race? Thee, chief, O Thames!
On whose each tide, glad with returning sails,
Flows in the mingled harvest of mankind?
And thee, thou Severn, whose prodigious swell
And waves resounding imitate the main?
Why need I name her deep capacious ports,
That point around the world? and why her seas?
All ocean is her own, and every land
To whom her ruling thunder ocean bears.
She too the mineral feeds—the obedient lead;
The warlike iron, nor the peaceful less,
Forming of life art-civilized the bond;
And that the Tyrian merchant sought of old,
Not dreaming then of Britain's brighter fame.
She rears to freedom an undaunted race:
Compatriot zealous, hospitable, kind,
Hers the warm Cambrian; hers the lofty Scot,
To hardship tamed, active in arts and arms,
Fired with a restless, an impatient flame,
That leads him raptured where ambition calls;
And English merit hers—where meet combined
Whate'er high fancy, sound judicious thought,
An ample generous heart, undrooping soul,
And firm tenacious valour can bestow.
Great nurse of fruits, of flocks, of commerce, she!
Great nurse of men! by thee, O Goddess, taught,
Her old renown I trace, disclose her source
Of wealth, of grandeur, and to Britons sing
A strain the muses never touched before.

'But how shall this thy mighty kingdom stand?
On what unyielding base? how finished shine?'

At this her eye, collecting all its fire,
Beamed more than human; and her awful voice
Majestic thus she raised: 'To Britons bear go
This closing strain, and with intenser note
Loud let it sound in their awakened ear:—
'On virtue can alone my kingdom stand,

On public virtue, every virtue joined.
For, lost this social cement of mankind,
The greatest empires by scarce-felt degrees
Will moulder soft away, till, tottering loose,
They prone at last to total ruin rush.
Unblessed by virtue, government a league
Becomes, a circling junto of the great,
To rob by law; religion mild, a yoke
To tame the stooping soul, a trick of state
To mask their rapine, and to share the prey.
What are without it senates, save a face
Of consultation deep and reason free,
While the determined voice and heart are sold?
What boasted freedom, save a sounding name?
And what election, but a market vile
Of slaves self-bartered? Virtue! without thee,
There is no ruling eye, no nerve, in states;
War has no vigour, and no safety peace:
Even justice warps to party, laws oppress,
Wide through the land their weak protection fails,
First broke the balance, and then scorned the sword.
Thus nations sink, society dissolves;
Rapine and guile and violence break loose,
Everting life, and turning love to gall;
Man hates the face of man, and Indian woods
And Libya's hissing sands to him are tame.

'By those three virtues be the frame sustained
Of British freedom—independent life;
Integrity in office; and, o'er all
Supreme, a passion for the commonweal.

'Hail! independence, hail! heaven's next best gift
To that of life and an immortal soul!
The life of life! that to the banquet high
And sober meal gives taste; to the bowed roof
Fair-dreamed repose, and to the cottage charms.
Of public freedom, hail, thou secret source!
Whose streams, from every quarter confluent, form
My better Nile, that nurses human life.
By rills from thee deduced, irriguous, fed,
The private field looks gay, with nature's wealth
Abundant flows, and blooms with each delight
That nature craves. Its happy master there,
The only freeman, walks his pleasing round—
Sweet-featured peace attending; fearless truth;
Firm resolution; goodness, blessing all
That can rejoice; contentment, surest friend;

And, still fresh stores from nature's book derived,
Philosophy, companion ever new.
These cheer his rural, and sustain or fire,
When into action called, his busy hours.
Meantime true-judging moderate desires,
Economy and taste, combined, direct
His clear affairs, and from debauching fiends
Secure his little kingdom. Nor can those
Whom fortune heaps, without these virtues, reach
That truce with pain, that animated ease,
That self-enjoyment springing from within,
That independence, active or retired,
Which make the soundest bliss of man below:
But, lost beneath the rubbish of their means,
And drained by wants to nature all unknown,
A wandering, tasteless, gaily wretched train,
Though rich, are beggars, and though noble, slaves.

'Lo! damned to wealth, at what a gross expense
They purchase disappointment, pain, and shame.
Instead of hearty hospitable cheer,
See how the hall with brutal riot flows;
While, in the foaming flood fermenting steeped,
The country maddens into party rage.
Mark those disgraceful piles of wood and stone;
Those parks and gardens, where, his haunts betrimmed,
And nature by presumptuous art oppressed,
The woodland genius mourns. See the full board
That steams disgust, and bowls that give no joy!
No truth invited there to feed the mind,
Nor wit the wine-rejoicing reason quaffs.
Hark how the dome with insolence resounds!
With those retained by vanity to scare
Repose and friends. To tyrant fashion, mark
The costly worship paid, to the broad gaze
Of fools! From still delusive day to day,
Led an eternal round of lying hope,
See, self-abandoned, how they roam adrift
Dashed o'er the town, a miserable wreck!
Then to adore some warbling eunuch turned,
With Midas' ears they crowd; or to the buzz
Of masquerade unblushing; or, to show
Their scorn of nature, at the tragic scene
They mirthful sit, or prove the comic true.
But, chief, behold around the rattling board,
The civil robbers ranged! and even the fair,
The tender fair, each sweetness laid aside,
As fierce for plunder as all-licensed troops

In some sacked city. Thus dissolved their wealth,
Without one generous luxury dissolved,
Or quartered on it many a needless want,
At the thronged levee bends the venal tribe;
With fair but faithless smiles each varnished o'er,
Each smooth as those that mutually deceive;
And for their falsehood each despising each;
Till, shook their patron by the wintry winds,
Wide flies the withered shower, and leaves him bare.
O far superior Afric's sable sons
By merchant pilfered to these willing slaves!
And rich as unsqueezed favourite to them
Is he who can his virtue boast alone!

'Britons! be firm; nor let corruption sly
Twine round your heart indissoluble chains.
The steel of Brutus burst the grosser bonds
By Caesar cast o'er Rome; but still remained
The soft enchanting fetters of the mind,
And other Caesars rose. Determined, hold
Your independence; for, that once destroyed,
Unfounded, freedom is a morning dream
That flits aerial from the spreading eye.

'Forbid it, Heaven! that ever I need urge
Integrity in office on my sons;
Inculcate common honour—not to rob;
And whom? the gracious, the confiding hand,
That lavishly rewards; the toiling poor,
Whose cup with many a bitter drop is mixed,
The guardian public, every face they see,
And every friend,—nay, in effect themselves.
As in familiar life the villain's fate
Admits no cure; so, when a desperate age
At this arrives, I the devoted race
Indignant spurn, and hopeless soar away.

'But, ah, too little known to modern times!
Be not the noblest passion passed unsung,
That ray peculiar, from unbounded love
Effused, which kindles the heroic soul—
Devotion to the public. Glorious flame!
Celestial ardour! in what unknown worlds,
Profusely scattered through the blue immense,
Hast thou been blessing myriads, since in Rome,
Old virtuous Rome, so many deathless names
From thee their lustre drew? since, taught by thee,
Their poverty put splendour to the blush,

Pain grew luxurious, and even death delight?
O wilt thou ne'er, in thy long period, look,
With blaze direct, on this my last retreat?

"Tis not enough, from self right—understood
Reflected, that thy rays inflame the heart:
Though virtue not disdains appeals to self,
Dreads not the trial; all her joys are true,
Nor is there any real joy save hers.
Far less the tepid, the declaiming race,
Foes to corruption, to its wages friends,
Or those whom private passions, for a while,
Beneath my standard list, can they suffice
To raise and fix the glory of my reign!

'An active flood of universal love
Must swell the breast. First, in effusion wide,
The restless spirit roves creation round,
And seizes every being; stronger then
It tends to life, whate'er the kindred search
Of bliss allies; then, more collected still,
It urges human kind; a passion grown,
At last the central parent public calls
Its utmost effort forth, awakes each sense,
The comely, grand, and tender. Without this,
This awful pant, shook from sublimer powers
Than those of self, this heaven-infused delight,
This moral gravitation, rushing prone
To press the public good, my system soon,
Traverse, to several selfish centres drawn,
Will reel to ruin—while for ever shut
Stand the bright portals of desponding fame.

'From sordid self shoot up no shining deeds,
None of those ancient lights that gladden earth,
Give grace to being, and arouse the brave
To just ambition, virtue's quickening fire!
Life tedious grows, an idly bustling round,
Filled up with actions animal and mean,
A dull gazette! The impatient reader scorns
The poor historic page; till kindly comes
Oblivion, and redeems a people's shame.
Not so the times when, emulation-stung,
Greece shone in genius, science, and in arts,
And Rome in virtues dreadful to be told!
To live was glory then! and charmed mankind,
Through the deep periods of devolving time,
Those, raptured, copy; these, astonished, read.

'True, a corrupted state, with every vice
And every meanness foul, this passion damps.
Who can unshocked behold the cruel eye?
The pale inveigling smile? the ruffian front?
The wretch abandoned to relentless self,
Equally vile if miser or profuse?
Powers not of God, assiduous to corrupt?
The fell deputed tyrant, who devours
The poor and weak, at distance from redress?
Delirious faction bellowing loud my name?
The false fair-seeming patriot's hollow boast?
A race resolved on bondage, fierce for chains,
My sacred rights a merchandise alone
Esteeming, and to work their feeder's will
By deeds, a horror to mankind, prepared,
As were the dregs of Romulus of old?
Who these indeed can undetesting see?—
But who unpitying? to the generous eye
Distress is virtue; and, though self-betrayed,
A people struggling with their fate must rouse
The hero's throb. Nor can a land at once
Be lost to virtue quite. How glorious then!
Fit luxury for gods! to save the good,
Protect the feeble, dash bold vice aside,
Depress the wicked, and restore the frail.
Posterity, besides—the young are pure,
And sons may tinge their father's cheek with shame.

'Should then the times arrive (which Heaven avert!)
That Britons bend unnerved, not by the force
Of arms, more generous and more manly, quelled,
But by corruption's soul-dejecting arts,
Arts impudent and gross! by their own gold,
In part bestowed to bribe them to give all;
With party raging, or immersed in sloth,
Should they Britannia's well fought laurels yield
To slily conquering Gaul, even from her brow
Let her own naval oak be basely torn
By such as tremble at the stiffening gale,
And nerveless sink while others sing rejoiced;
Or (darker prospect! scarce one gleam behind
Disclosing) should the broad corruptive plague
Breathe from the city to the farthest hut
That sits serene within the forest shade,
The fevered people fire, inflame their wants
And their luxurious thirst, so gathering rage
That, were a buyer found, they stand prepared

To sell their birthright for a cooling draught;
Should shameless pens for plain corruption plead,
The hired assassins of the commonweal!
Deemed the declaiming rant of Greece and Rome;
Should public virtue grow the public scoff,
Till private, failing, staggers through the land—
Till round the city loose mechanic want,
Dire-prowling nightly, makes the cheerful haunts
Of men more hideous than Numidian wilds,
Nor from its fury sleeps the vale in peace,
And murders, horrors, perjuries abound—
Nay, till to lowest deeds the highest stoop,
The rich, like starving wretches, thirst for gold,
And those on whom the vernal showers of heaven
All-bounteous fall and that prime lot bestow,
A power to live to nature and themselves,
In sick attendance wear their anxious days
With fortune joyless, and with honours mean:
Meantime, perhaps, profusion flows around,
The waste of war without the works of peace,
No mark of millions in the gulf absorbed
Of uncreating vice, none but the rage
Of roused corruption still demanding more:
That very portion which (by faithful skill
Employed) might make the smiling public rear
Her ornamented head, drilled through the hands
Of mercenary tools, serves but to nurse
A locust band within, and in the bud
Leaves starved each work of dignity and use:

'I paint the worst; but should these times arrive,
If any nobler passion yet remain,
Let all my sons all parties fling aside,
Despise their nonsense, and together join;
Let worth and virtue scorning low despair,
Exerted full, from every quarter shine
Commixed in heightened blaze. Light flashed to light,
Moral or intellectual, more intense
By giving glows—as, on pure winter's eve,
Gradual the stars effulge; fainter, at first,
They straggling rise, but, when the radiant host,
In thick profusion poured, shine out immense,
Each casting vivid influence on each,
From pole to pole a glittering deluge plays
And worlds above rejoice and men below.

'But why to Britons this superfluous strain?—
Good nature, honest truth even somewhat blunt,

Of crooked baseness an indignant scorn,
A zeal unyielding in their country's cause,
And ready bounty, wont to dwell with them:
Nor only wont-wide o'er the land diffused,
In many a blest retirement still they dwell.

'To softer prospect turn we now the view,
To laurelled science, arts, and public works,
That lend my finished fabric comely pride,
Grandeur and grace. Of sullen genius he!
Cursed by the muses! by the graces loathed!
Who deems beneath the public's high regard
These last enlivening touches of my reign.
However puffed with power and gorged with wealth
A nation be; let trade enormous rise,
Let East and South their mingled treasure pour
Till, swelled impetuous, the corrupting flood
Burst o'er the city and devour the land—
Yet, these neglected, these recording arts,
Wealth rots, a nuisance; and, oblivious sunk,
That nation must another Carthage lie.
If not by them, on monumental brass,
On sculptured marble, on the deathless page
Impressed, renown had left no trace behind;
In vain, to future times, the sage had thought,
The legislator planned, the hero found
A beauteous death, the patriot toiled in vain.
The awarders they of fame's immortal wreath!
They rouse ambition, they the mind exalt,
Give great ideas, lovely forms infuse,
Delight the general eye, and, dressed by them,
The moral Venus glows with double charms.

'Science, my close associate, still attends
Where'er I go. Sometimes, in simple guise,
She walks the furrow with the consul-swain.
Whispering unlettered wisdom to the heart
Direct; or sometimes, in the pompous robe
Of fancy dressed, she charms Athenian wits,
And a whole sapient city round her burns.
Then o'er her brow Minerva's terrors nod:
With Xenophon, sometimes, in dire extremes
She breathes deliberate soul, and makes retreat
Unequalled glory: with the Theban sage,
Epaminondas, first and best of men!
Sometimes she bids the deep-embattled host,
Above the vulgar reach resistless formed,
March to sure conquest—never gained before!

Nor on the treacherous seas of giddy state
Unskilful she: when the triumphant tide
Of high-swoln empire wears one boundless smile,
And the gale tempts to new pursuits of fame,
Sometimes, with Scipio, she collects her sail,
And seeks the blissful shore of rural ease
Where, but the Aonian maids, no sirens sing;
Or, should the deep-brewed tempest muttering rise,
While rocks and shoals perfidious lurk around,
With Tully she her wide-reviving light
To senates holds, a Catiline confounds,
And saves awhile from Caesar sinking Rome.
Such the kind power whose piercing eye dissolves
Each mental fetter and sets reason free;
For me inspiring an enlightened zeal,
The more tenacious as the more convinced
How happy freemen, and how wretched slaves.
To Britons not unknown, to Britons full
The Goddess spreads her stores, the secret soul
That quickens trade, the breath unseen that wafts
To them the treasures of a balanced world.
But finer arts (save what the muse has sung
In daring flight, above all modern wing)
Neglected droop the head; and public works,
Broke by corruption into private gain,
Not ornament, disgrace—not serve, destroy.

'Shall Britons, by their own joint wisdom ruled
Beneath one royal head, whose vital power
Connects, enlivens, and exerts the whole;
In finer arts, and public works, shall they
To Gallia yield? yield to a land that bends,
Depressed and broke, beneath the will of one?
Of one who, should the unkingly thirst of gold,
Or tyrant passions, or ambition prompt,
Calls locust-armies o'er the blasted land,
Drains from its thirsty bounds the springs of wealth
His own insatiate reservoir to fill,
To the lone desert patriot-merit frowns,
Or into dungeons arts, when they, their chains
Indignant bursting, for their nobler works
All other licence scorn but truth's and mine.
Oh shame to think! shall Britons, in the field
Unconquered still, the better laurel lose?
Even in that monarch's reign who vainly dreamt,
By giddy power betrayed and flattered pride,
To grasp unbounded sway; while, swarming round,
His armies dared all Europe to the field;

To hostile hands while treasure flowed profuse,
And, that great source of treasure, subjects' blood,
Inhuman squandered, sickened every land;
From Britain, chief, while my superior sons,
In vengeance rushing, dashed his idle hopes,
And bade his agonizing heart be low:
Even then, as in the golden calm of peace,
What public works, at home, what arts arose!
What various science shone! what genius glowed!
"Tis not for me to paint, diffusive shot
O'er fair extents of land, the shining road;
The flood-compelling arch; the long canal,
Through mountains piercing and uniting seas;
The dome resounding sweet with infant joy,
From famine saved, or cruel-handed shame;
And that where valour counts his noble scars;
The land where social pleasure loves to dwell,
Of the fierce demon, Gothic duel, freed;
The robber from his farthest forest chased;
The turbid city cleared and by degrees
Into sure peace, the best police, refined,
Magnificence, and grace, and decent joy.
Let Gallic bards record how honoured arts
And science, by despotic bounty blessed,
At distance flourished from my parent-eye;
Restoring ancient taste how Boileau rose;
How the big Roman soul shook in Corneille
The trembling stage; in elegant Racine
How the more powerful though more humble voice
Of nature-painting Greece resistless breathed
The whole awakened heart; how Moliere's scene,
Chastised and regular, with well judged wit,
Not scattered wild, and native humour graced,
Was life itself; to public honours raised,
How learning in warm seminaries spread,
And, more for glory than the small reward,
How emulation strove; how their pure tongue
Almost obtained what was denied their arms;
From Rome, awhile, how painting, courted long,
With Poussin came—ancient design, that lifts
A fairer front and looks another soul;
How the kind art, that, of unvalued price,
The famed and only picture easy gives,
Refined her touch, and through the shadowed piece
All the live spirit of the painter poured;
Coyest of arts, how sculpture northward deigned
A look, and bade her Girardon arise;
How lavish grandeur blazed, the barren waste

Astonished saw the sudden palace swell,
And fountains spout amid its arid shades;
For leagues, bright vistas opening to the view,
How forests in majestic gardens smiled;
How menial arts, by their gay sisters taught,
Wove the deep flower, the blooming foliage trained
In joyous figures o'er the silky lawn,
The palace cheered, illumed the storied wall,
And with the pencil vied the glowing loom.
'These laurels, Louis, by the droppings raised
Of thy profusion, its dishonour shade,
And green through future times shall bind thy brow;
While the vain honours of perfidious war
Wither, abhorred or in oblivion lost.
With what prevailing vigour had they shot,
And stole a deeper root, by the full tide
Of war-sunk millions fed? Superior still,
How had they branched luxuriant to the skies
In Britain planted, by the potent juice
Of freedom swelled? Forced is the bloom of arts,
A false uncertain spring, when bounty gives,
Weak without me, a transitory gleam.
Fair shine the slippery days, enticing skies
Of favour smile, and courtly breezes blow;
Till arts, betrayed, trust to the flattering air
Their tender blossom: then malignant rise
The blights of envy, of those insect clouds,
That, blasting merit, often cover courts.
Nay, should, perchance, some kind Maecenas aid
The doubtful beamings of his prince's soul,
His wavering ardour fix, and unconfined
Diffuse his warm beneficence around;
Yet death, at last, and wintry tyrants come,
Each sprig of genius killing at the root.
But, when with me imperial bounty joins,
Wide o'er the public blows eternal spring;
While mingled autumn every harvest pours
Of every land, whate'er invention, art,
Creating toil, and nature can produce.'

Here ceased the Goddess; and her ardent wings,
Dipped in the colours of the heavenly bow,
Stood waving radiance round, for sudden flight
Prepared, when thus impatient burst my prayer:
'O forming light of life! O better sun!
Sun of mankind! by whom the cloudy north,
Sublimed, not envies Languedocian skies
That, unstained ether all, diffusive smile—

When shall we call these ancient laurels ours?
And when thy work complete?' Straight with her hand,
Celestial red, she touched my darkened eyes.
As at the touch of day the shades dissolve,
So quick, methought, the misty circle cleared
That dims the dawn of being here below;
The future shone disclosed, and, in long view,
Bright rising eras instant rushed to light.

'They come! great Goddess! I the times behold!
The times our fathers in the bloody field
Have earned so dear, and, not with less renown,
In the warm struggles of the senate-fight.
The times I see whose glory to supply,
For toiling ages, commerce round the world
Has winged unnumbered sails and from each land
Materials heaped that, well employed, with Rome
Might vie our grandeur, and with Greece our art!

'Lo! princes I behold! contriving still,
And still conducting firm some brave design;
Kings! that the narrow joyless circle scorn.
Burst the blockade of false designing men,
Of treacherous smiles, of adulation fell,
And of the blinding clouds around them thrown:
Their court rejoicing millions; worth, alone,
And virtue dear to them; their best delight,
In just proportion, to give general joy;
Their jealous care thy kingdom to maintain;
The public glory theirs; unsparing love
Their endless treasure, and their deeds their praise.
With thee they work. Nought can resist your force:
Life feels it quickening in her dark retreats:
Strong spread the blooms of genius, science, art;
His bashful bounds disclosing merit breaks;
And, big with fruits of glory, virtue blows
Expansive o'er the land. Another race
Of generous youth, of patriot sires, I see!
Not those vain insects fluttering in the blaze
Of court, and ball, and play—those venal souls,
Corruption's veteran unrelenting bands,
That, to their vices slaves, can ne'er be free.

'I see the fountains purged! whence life derives
A clear or turbid flow; see the young mind
Not fed impure by chance, by flattery fooled,
Or by scholastic jargon bloated proud,
But filled and nourished by the light of truth.

Then, beamed through fancy the refining ray,
And, pouring on the heart, the passions feel
At once informing light and moving flame;
Till moral, public, graceful action crowns
The whole. Behold! the fair contention glows
In all that mind or body can adorn
And form to life. Instead of barren heads,
Barbarian pedants, wrangling sons of pride,
And truth-perplexing metaphysic wits,
Men, patriots, chiefs, and citizens are formed.

'Lo! justice, like the liberal light of heaven,
Unpurchased shines on all; and from her beam,
Appalling guilt, retire the savage crew
That prowl amid the darkness they themselves
Have thrown around the laws. Oppression grieves:
See how her legal furies bite the lip
While Yorks and Talbots their deep snares detect,
And seize swift justice through the clouds they raise.

'See! social labour lifts his guarded head,
And men not yield to government in vain.
From the sure land is rooted ruffian force,
And the lewd nurse of villains, idle waste;
Lo! razed their haunts, down dashed their maddening bowl,
A nation's poison, beauteous order reigns!
Manly submission, unimposing toil,
Trade without guile, civility that marks
From the foul herd of brutal slaves thy sons,
And fearless peace. Or, should affronting war
To slow but dreadful vengeance rouse the just,
Unfailing fields of freemen I behold
That know with their own proper arm to guard
Their own blest isle against a leaguing world.
Despairing Gaul her boiling youth restrains,
Dissolved her dream of universal sway:
The winds and seas are Britain's wide domain,
And not a sail but by permission spreads.

'Lo! swarming southward on rejoicing suns
Gay colonies extend—the calm retreat
Of undeserved distress, the better home
Of those whom bigots chase from foreign lands;
Not built on rapine, servitude, and woe,
And in their turn some petty tyrant's prey,
But, bound by social freedom, firm they rise;
Such as, of late, an Oglethorpe has formed,
And, crowding round, the charmed Savannah sees.

'Horrid with want and misery, no more
Our streets the tender passenger afflict.
Nor shivering age, nor sickness without friend
Or home or bed to bear his burning load,
Nor agonizing infant, that ne'er earned
Its guiltless pangs, I see! The stores profuse
Which British bounty has to these assigned
No more the sacrilegious riot swell
Of cannibal devourers! right applied,
No starving wretch the land of freedom stains—
If poor, employment finds; if old, demands,
If sick, if maimed, his miserable due;
And will, if young, repay the fondest care.
Sweet sets the sun of stormy life; and sweet
The morning shines, in mercy's dews arrayed.
Lo! how they rise! these families of heaven!
That, chief, (but why, ye bigots! why so late?)
Where blooms and warbles glad a rising age;
What smiles of praise! And, while their song ascends,
The listening seraph lays his lute aside.

'Hark! the gay muses raise a nobler strain,
With active nature, warm impassioned truth,
Engaging fable, lucid order, notes
Of various string, and heart-felt image filled.
Behold! I see the dread delightful school
Of tempered passions and of polished life
Restored: behold! the well dissembled scene
Calls from embellished eyes the lovely tear,
Or lights up mirth in modest cheeks again.
Lo! vanished monster-land. Lo! driven away
Those that Apollo's sacred walks profane—
Their wild creation scattered, where a world
Unknown to nature, Chaos more confused,
O'er the brute scene its ouran-outangs pours;
Detested forms! that, on the mind impressed,
Corrupt, confound, and barbarize an age.

'Behold! all thine again the sister-arts,
Thy graces they, knit in harmonious dance.
Nursed by the treasure from a nation drained
Their works to purchase, they to nobler rouse
Their untamed genius, their unfettered thought;
Of pompous tyrants and of dreaming monks
The gaudy tools and prisoners no more.

'Lo! numerous domes a Burlington confess—

For kings and senates fit; the palace see!
The temple breathing a religious awe;
Even framed with elegance the plain retreat,
The private dwelling. Certain in his aim,
Taste, never idly working, saves expense.

'See! sylvan scenes, where art alone pretends
To dress her mistress and disclose her charms—
Such as a Pope in miniature has shown,
A Bathurst o'er the widening forest spreads,
And such as form a Richmond, Chiswick, Stowe.

'August around what public works I see!
Lo! stately streets, lo! squares that court the breeze;
In spite of those to whom pertains the care
Ingulfing more than founded Roman ways,
Lo! rayed from cities o'er the brightened land,
Connecting sea to sea, the solid road.
Lo! the proud arch (no vile exactor's stand)
With easy sweep bestrides the chasing flood.
See! long canals, and deepened rivers join
Each part with each, and with the circling main
The whole enlivened isle. Lo! ports expand,
Free as the winds and waves, their sheltering arms.
Lo! streaming comfort o'er the troubled deep,
On every pointed coast the lighthouse towers;
And, by the broad imperious mole repelled,
Hark! how the baffled storm indignant roars.'

As thick to view these varied wonders rose,
Shook all my soul with transport, unassured
The Vision broke; and on my waking eye
Rushed the still ruins of dejected Rome.

A CHRONOLOGY

TO ELUCIDATE AND ILLUSTRATE THE LIFE AND TIMES OF JAMES THOMSON

1666. Birth of Thomas Thomson, the poet's father. Minister of Ednam, Roxburghshire. 1693. Marries Beatrix, daughter of Alexander Trotter, of Widehope (a small lairdship in Roxburghshire).

1694. Birth of Voltaire.

1700. Birth, at Ednam or Widehope, of James Thomson, the poet—fourth child (third son) of his parents; born (probably) on the 7th, baptized on the 15th of September. In the November following, his father inducted into the parish of Southdean, Roxburghshire. Birth of David Malloch (or Mallet). Death of Dryden.

1709. Birth of Johnson. 1712. Young Thomson attends a Grammar School in Jedburgh, some eight miles or so from Southdean. His acquaintance with Mr. (afterwards the Rev.) Robert Riccaltoun, farmer at Earlshaugh, begins about this time. First attempts at versifying, a year or two later.

1715. Young Thomson enters Edinburgh University.

1716. Death of his father, in February, while exorcizing a ghost. Home transferred to Edinburgh.

1719. Death of Addison.

1720. Thomson now a student of Divinity. Continues versifying, chiefly on rural subjects in the heroic couplet; contributes to The Edinburgh Miscellany Of a Country Life, &c.

1721. Birth of Collins. Walpole Prime Minister (till 1742).

1724. Thomson still at the University. Adverse criticism, by the Professor of Divinity, of one of his college exercises (a discourse on the 10th portion of Psalm cxix), the turning-point of his life.

1725. End of February, Thomson sets out to seek his fortune in London: embarks at Leith, not again to see Scotland. Visits Drury Lane Theatre, and sees Gato acted. Death of his mother, in May. In July, acting as tutor to Lord Binning's son, at Barnet, near London. Composition of Winter in the following autumn and winter. Publication of Allan Ramsay's The Gentle Shepherd.

1726. I March, Winter, a thin folio of 16 pp., 40511., price 18., John Millan, publisher. Dyer's Grongar Hill published. Thomson acting as tutor in an academy in London. Acquaintance with Aaron Hill. Second edition of Winter, in June.

1727. Death of Sir Isaac Newton: in June, Thomson publishes a poem To the Memory of Newton. Summer published; a second edition the same year. Thomson now relying on literature for his support. Britannia written (not published till 1729), in opposition to the peace-at-any-price policy of Walpole. The poet spends part of the summer at Marlborough Castle (the guest of the Countess of Hertford).

1728. Spring published by Andrew Millar. Goldsmith born.

1729. Death of Congreve: anonymous poem To the Memory of Congreve published; attributed to Thomson on very unsatisfactory evidence. In September, Thomson the guest of Bubb Dodington at Eastbury. The poet busy in various ways—with the tragedy of Sophonisba, the completion of The Seasons, the publication of Britannia, and contributions to Ralph's, Miscellany; among the last a Hymn, on Solitude, The Happy Man, and a metrical version of a passage of St. Matthew's Gospel.

1730. Publication of the first collected edition of The Seasons (including Autumn and the Hymn for the first time): two editions, one in quarto at a guinea, published by subscription; the other in octavo. Sophonisba produced at Drury Lane, February 28th, Mrs. Oldfield taking the part of the heroine: a success on the stage, despite one weak line, and selling well when printed. Travelling tutor to young

Charles Talbot, son of Mr. Charles Talbot, then Solicitor-General (soon afterwards Lord Chancellor); in Paris in December, where (probably) he visits Voltaire.

1731. Visits most of the courts and capital cities of Europe (Murdoch); in Paris in October. Visits Italy—'I long to see the fields where Virgil gathered his immortal honey,' &c. Collecting material for his poem on Liberty. Correspondence with Dodington—' Should you inquire after my muse, I believe she did not cross the Channel with me.' Probably wrote, however, the lines on the death of Aikman, the painter. Returns to England in December. Birth of Cowper. The Gentleman's Magazine established.

1733. Death of young Talbot in September; the elder becomes Lord Chancellor in November; soon after, Thomson appointed Secretary of Briefs in the Court of Chancery—the post a sinecure with about 300l. a year. Some personal stanzas of The Castle of Indolence written about this time.

1735. Publication of Liberty; Parts I, II, and III, at intervals.

1736. Liberty, Parts IV and V at intervals. Thomson goes to live in Kew Lane, Richmond—his residence for the rest of his life. Intimacy with Pope, whose house was only a mile off, at Twickenham. Busy with the drama—'whipping and spurring to finish a tragedy this winter.' Sends pecuniary assistance to his sisters in Edinburgh. Becomes acquainted with 'Amanda'.

1737. Death of Lord Chancellor Talbot, in February; Thomson's memorial verses (panegyric and elegy) in June. Writing Agamemnon. Loss of Secretaryship. Acquaintance with George Lyttelton. Pension of 100l. a year from the Prince of Wales, to whom Liberty had been dedicated. Shenstone's Schoolmistress published.

1738. Thomson's Preface to Milton's Areopagitica appears. Agamemnon produced in April, Quin in the title role. A new edition (a reprint of octavo edition of 1730) of The Seasons brought out.

1739. Thomson's tragedy of Edward and Eleonora prohibited by the censorship.

1740. Conjointly with Malloch, The Masque of Alfred, containing the ode 'Rule, Britannia', performed August 1, in Clifden Gardens, before the Prince of Wales. 1742. Young's Night thoughts (Books I-III). 1743. Visits the Lytteltons, at Hagley Park, in August—'I am come to the most agreeable place and company in the world.' Correspondence with 'Amanda'.—' But wherever I am... I never cease to think of my loveliest Miss Young. You are part of my being; you mix with all my thoughts.' His song, For ever, Fortune, wilt thou prove, ' about this time. Preparing, at Hagley, a revised edition of The Seasons with Lyttelton's assistance.

1744. New edition of The Seasons, with many alterations and additions. Lyttelton in office: he appoints Thomson Surveyor-General of the Leeward Islands—a sinecure post, worth 300l. a year clear. Death of Pope.

1745. His best drama Tancred and Sigismunda produced at Drury Lane, with Garrick as Tancred. At Hagley in the summer.

1746. Thomson makes way for his friend (and deputy), William Paterson, in the office of Surveyor-General. At Hagley in the autumn. Last edition of The Seasons published in the poet's lifetime. Collins's Odes published.

1747. At Hagley in the autumn. Visits Shenstone at the Leasowes. Busy at Coriolanus (nearly finished in March).

1748. Prince of Wales's displeasure with Lyttelton visited on Lyttelton's friends—Thomson's name struck off pension list. The Castle of Indolence, in May. Death of Thomson, after short illness, at Richmond, August 27th. Buried in Richmond churchyard. Collins's Ode in memory of Thomson—a lasting memorial.

1749. Coriolanus produced, in January—the Prologue by Lyttelton.

1753. Shiels's Life of Thomson (Cibber's Life of the Poets)

1758. Death of Allan Ramsay.

1759. Birth of Burns.

1762. Murdoch's Memoir of Thomson (prefixed to an edition of Thomson's Works). Monument to Thomson in Westminster Abbey.

1781. Johnson's Life of Thomson (Lives of the Poets).

1791. Burns's Address to the Shade of Thomson.

1792. The Earl of Buchan's Essay on the Life of the Poet Thomson

1831. Biography of Thomson by Sir Harris Nicholas (prefixed to the Aldine Edition of Thomson's Works: annotated by P, Cunningham, 1860).

1842. An edition of The Seasons, with notes by Bolton Corney.

1891. Clarendon Press edition of The Seasons and The Castle of Indolence, with a biographical notice and full notes by J. Logie Robertson.

1894. Furth in Field (Part IV—On the poet of The Seasons), by Hugh Haliburton.

1895. James Thomson: Sa Vie et ses Oeuvres (678 pp.), by Leon Morel.

1898. James Thomson (in Famous Scots Series), by W. Bayne.

1908. James Thomson (in English Men of Letters Series), by G. C. Macaulay.

www.ingramcontent.com/pod-product-compliance
Lightning Source LLC
Chambersburg PA
CBHW021933040426
42448CB00008B/1037